Buying and Renovating a Property in France

If you want to know how . . .

Going to Live in France
Your practical guide to life and work in France

Going to Live in Paris
Your practical guide to living and working in France's capital

Buying a Property in France
An insider guide to realising your dream

Starting & Running a B&B in France
How to make money and enjoy a new lifestyle running your own chambres d'hôtes

Retire Abroad
Your complete guide to a new life in the sun

howtobooks

For full details, please send for a free copy of the latest catalogue to:
How To Books
3 Newtec Place, Magdalen Road
Oxford OX4 1RE, United Kingdom
info@howtobooks.co.uk
www.howtobooks.co.uk

The Daily Telegraph

Buying and Renovating a Property in France

RICHARD WHITING

howtobooks

Published by How To Books Ltd,
3 Newtec Place, Magdalen Road,
Oxford OX4 1RE, United Kingdom.
Tel: (01865) 793806. Fax: (01865) 248780.
email: info@howtobooks.co.uk
www.howtobooks.co.uk

First published 2004

British Library Cataloguing in Publication Data
A catalogue record for this book is available from
the British Library

Cover design by Baseline Arts Ltd, Oxford
Illustrations by Nicki Averill
Produced for How To Books by Deer Park Productions, Tavistock
Typeset by TW Typesetting, Plymouth, Devon
Printed and bound by Bell & Bain Ltd, Glasgow

NOTE: The material contained in this book is set out in good faith for general guidance
and no liability can be accepted for loss or expense incurred as a result of relying in
particular circumstances on statements made in the book. Laws and regulations are
complex and liable to change, and readers should check the current position with the
relevant authorities before making personal arrangements.

Contents

Note from the author   xi

Part One: First Considerations

1 **Being Clear About Your Aims**   **3**
  What are you planning to do?   3
  Premises for rental or other business purposes   4

2 **Some Typical and Not So Typical Conversions, Renovations**
  and Restorations   **7**
  Britanny   8
  Case study – a *longère*; The dining room and lounge; The kitchen; The garden;
  Other properties
  Lower Normandy   10
  Case study – a *pressoir*; The living room and sitting room; The kitchen;
  A special bedroom and bathroom
  Upper Savoy   13
  Case study – a chalet; The ground floor; The large lounge, small sitting room,
  dining room, kitchen and master bedroom; Under the eaves
  Provence   15
  Case study – a *mas* farmhouse; The kitchen; The lounge and dining room;
  An attic bedroom and a retro style bathroom; The swimming pool and garden
  Languedoc-Roussillon   18
  Case study – a *relais*; The dining room; The patio and winter-garden;
  The upstairs bedrooms; Final note; Other properties
  Finally   21

3 **Location, Position and Outlook**   **23**
  Factors to consider   23
  Typical properties in different regions   24
  Top prices; Properties offering numerous possibilities; Farm buildings (*corps de
  ferme*), more than a *fermette*; Atlantic coast *départements* – holiday/letting
  property and an unfinished property; Various properties in the Centre region
  (Loire Valley)

4 **Estate Agents, Visiting Properties and the Buying Procedure** **28**
  Property prospecting   29
  English-language property magazines   29

French property magazines and websites   29

French property shows in the UK   31

Visiting properties   32
Signing a *bon de visite*; Property descriptions; Estate agents; Points to check;
Estate agents' fees; Notaries' fees

Property auctions   37

Private sales   38

Buying your property   39
Compromis de vente; *Promesse unilatérale de vente*; Cooling-off period;
The notary's tasks; *Acte de vente définitive*; Notary charges (*frais de notaire*);
Droits d'enregistrement et taxes; *Emoluments de notaire*

5   Understanding the Regulations   **44**

Local regulations   44

National regulations   45

Planning permission   48

Notification of work to be carried out (*déclaration de travaux*)   48

Part Two: Renovating Your Property

6   Extensions and Verandas   **53**

Extensions   54
Foundations; Walls; Windows; Ceilings and roofs; Heating

Verandas   58
Foundations; Choice of materials, heating and insulation

7   Conversions   **61**

Attics   62
Grenier (hay or grain-loft); *Combles* (attics); *Chambre de bonne* (garret); Heating,
insulation and soundproofing

Garage conversions   65

Basements   66
Problems with damp; Different uses of basements

Ground-level former stabling, cattle sheds, work floors or similar   68

Floor coverings   70
Main floor tile types; Laying flooring

8   Complete Transformation and Redesign   **73**

Using an architect   73

Demolition permits   74

Work completed report documents 75

Bedrooms 76

Kitchens 78

Bathrooms 84

Bathroom and kitchen floor and wall coverings 89

Doors 89

Windows 90

9 Renovation **92**

Roofing 93

Termites 95

Asbestos 96

Lead-content paints 97

Shutters 98
Maintaining shutters

Reviewing the electrical wiring 101
Your electricity tariff; Electrical circuits; Socket amperages and numbers;
French plugs; Safety regulations; Re-wiring and updating appliances

Heating options 105
Electrical heating; Gas central heating; Oil-fired central heating; Under-floor
heating; Log-burning fireplaces and stoves; Solar power

Alarm systems 111

The plumbing system 113
Pipe and tubing materials most frequently used; Mains drainage and septic tanks

10 Restoration **118**

Enamelware 119

Fireplaces 120

Floor tiles 120

Wall tiles 121

Shutters 121

Staircases 121

Wooden doors and ceiling beams 122

Ravalement 122

11 Redecoration **125**

Using an *artisan peintre* 126

Employing a *décorateur* 126

Preparation 127
Materials 128
Undercoats and roughcast coatings for interiors; Cork, wood-panel strips
and made-up wood slabs; Paints; Wallpaper and wall fabrics

12 Outhouses, Swimming Pools and Terraces **133**
Outhouses 133
Stone shed outhouses; Larger outhouses
Swimming pools 135
Utility; Position; Size; Safety; Construction type and guarantee; Some technical
terms; Cost and value; Appearance; Maintenance
Terraces 140
Foundations

Part Three: Practical Advice

13 Basic Materials and Tools **147**
Where to buy DIY products 148
General maintenance 148
Tools 149
Specialised equipment 152

14 Companies, Materials and Shopping Around **153**
Building companies 154
Qualibat; *Maître Artisan*; *Cheque Emploi Service*; *Qualifelec*; English-speaking
companies
Building materials 155
NF products; *Certificats CSTBat*; Acotherm; 'Private labels'
Shopping around 156
DIY, architect or professional contractor? 158

15 Cost, Finance, VAT and Taxation **160**
Cost 160
Estimates
Finance 162
Le prêt conventionné (PC); *Crédit immobilier bancaire* (bank property loan);
Prêts bancaires personnels (personal bank loans); *Le prêt pass-travaux*;
Loans for gas and electrical work; Solar energy; Store finance offers
VAT (*TVA*) 166

Taxation   168
Taxe foncière (land tax); *Taxe d'habitation* (community tax); *Taxe locale d'équipement* (town planning tax); *Le credit d'impôt*; Robien's tax relief measure

Useful Websites   **172**

Further Reading   **176**

Index   **177**

Note from the Author

This book aims to give you sufficient suggestions and practical advice and information to make your purchase and renovation in France a pleasure and not a chore. Not least important is its intention to help you avoid making a disastrous purchase: regulations or the topography prevent you from renovating as you intended or laying on utility services, or the property is unsound. It should be read entirely before dipping into any topics for specific information as it has not been written as a manual.

You are already 'sold' on France but are perhaps undecided whether to buy a *neuf* (up to five years old) or an *ancien* (over five years old) property which requires renovation. Or, at the end of the buying process, you may have completed your *ancien* purchase and are considering how best to renovate.

Just over 900,000 properties were purchased in France in 2002, a quite exceptional year, and 70 per cent of these were in the *ancien* category, which includes the great majority of properties advertised as *à renover* (requiring renovation), *prévoir travaux* (work required) or *à aménager* (with conversion possibilities). The *FNAIM*, The French National Federation of Estate Agents, have just reported (January 2004) an important average price increase in 2003 of 14.2% in *ancien* property prices. There was, however, a slight reduction in sales, of 2%, in 2003 in this category compared to 2002. Properties for renovation are, of course, by definition at the lower end of the *ancien* price ranges. Low-cost flights from the UK to various parts of France appear to be here to stay, helping to make the choice of which region to live in much wider than the traditional renovated-property strongholds of Brittany and Normandy.

Your initial search, whether you're set on buying a *maison de village* (an old village cottage or house), a *fermette* (small farmhouse), a *maison de maître* (a fine town or country residence) or a specialty such as a former oil mill, water mill or windmill may mean several trips. If you're not immediately resident in the property, keeping an eye on any major work to be done, even if you're employing a local architect as the supervisory *maître d'oeuvre*, may mean frequent visits. You may also wish to visit the UK regularly if you are making the property your all-year-round home.

Location is always a key element in a property purchase. And especially so where property renovations are concerned in France. It may seem quite evident, but is the location subject to an Alpine, Atlantic, Continental or Mediterranean climate? Each climate is quite different and their extremes should, ideally, be experienced and taken into account prior to paying your 10 per cent deposit when you sign the *compromis de vente* (preliminary contract of sale). Will your budget match the work – including additional or replacement heating systems, air-conditioning, insulation, storm-proofing and/or wind-proofing – that may be required? Global warming over the last few years has seen prolonged heat-waves in the South of France and unexpected deluges and storms throughout France.

While the mechanics of the buying procedure are covered in Chapter 4 in the 'First Considerations' part of this book, the emphasis is on verification of the materials used in the property under consideration and on effective methods of prospecting which eliminate a lot of otherwise wasted time. If a property is advertised as 'genuine 18th century' ensure, for example, that this can be certified.

The 'First Considerations' section also has chapters on what may motivate the purchase, accounts of superb renovations, a detailed look at the importance of location, and the all-important local and national regulations for property alterations and planning permission.

This sets the scene for the 'bricks and mortar' part of the book, 'Renovating Your Property', which is designed to provide you with sufficient knowledge about French building methods and materials so that you can understand estimates and evaluate work that should only be done by professional companies approved by independent organisations. Personal safety, the solidity of the property and the *garantie décennale* (10 year guarantee) are all covered. This section looks at everything from full-scale conversions, renovations and restorations to terraces and verandas. Risk-free DIY jobs, even if you're not normally a handyman (or woman), are also described in this section.

The third and final part, 'Practical Advice', is designed to cut your costs wherever possible. It explains the best loans, tax advantages such as the recent *dispositif de Robien* (Robien's tax law) applicable under certain conditions to *ancien* properties, estimates, best buys for materials and tools and a reappraisal of the roles of architects and/or professional contractors. It is important here to know that conversion, improvement, renovation and transformation work carried out by professional builders to properties over two years old, and which has **not** created a new building, extension, veranda or other additional habitable floor area with a ceiling height of 1.80 m or over, has benefited from the greatly reduced VAT rate of 5.5 per cent since September 1999. The French government recently confirmed that this reduced rate will continue up until the end of 2005. This is another good reason for buying for renovation as soon as you can. Chapter 16 gives full details.

Inevitably in a book of this kind, some information on topics like walls, floors, heating, etc. is common to different chapters. We have tried to keep repetition to a minimum using cross-referencing. In some instances information that could well have been part of two chapters is given in only one chapter. For example, information on mains drainage and septic tanks is given in Chapter 9 (Renovation) under 'The plumbing system' although it could well have been part of Chapter 8 (Complete Transformation and Redesign).

Prices and approximate prices given for appliances, materials and building work are those known to be practiced or applied by manufacturers, suppliers or service companies. Negotiation is possible, of course, particularly as concerns estimates and purchases of authentic old or second-hand building materials.

A French-English dictionary reminding you of the words and expressions encountered in the text, and introducing you to some you will no doubt encounter, is at the end of each topic or chapter. While the euro symbol, €, is shown before amounts in the text, e.g. '€5,000', in the case of typical estimates the euro symbol is often afterwards, e.g. '300€', as it would be in French companies' estimates.

I would like to thank in particular Michel Segalen, who first took me on in his *agence immobilière* (estate agency company), and Betty Bloom of Spa Properties (Europe) in London who sent me my first UK enquiries. My thanks also go, in particular, to my brother-in-law, Pierre, who has put up with my curiosity over the years as he modified and renovated his house creating new rooms, a veranda, a swimming pool and a large fitted kitchen.

Richard Whiting

Part One

First Considerations

1

Being Clear About Your Aims

You may not have decided yet where you plan to buy and the type of property you envisage, but it is important to have a clear idea from the outset of the reasons for your purchase. Total fees that you, the *acquéreur* (buyer), must pay are between 10 and 15 per cent for a small or medium-size *ancien* property, to which you will probably be adding an architect or construction expert's fee and possibly that of a *géomètre expert* (chartered surveyor) before you start paying any renovation costs, so it is advisable to set your criteria down on paper as a 'Does it fit the bill?' checklist at this stage.

WHAT ARE YOU PLANNING TO DO?

Will you be moving, lock stock and barrel, to your 'new' permanent residence or are you seeking a holiday home which you will visit regularly but may also let out for holidays to other people? Are you looking for a sound capital investment, and a good rental return if the property is to be rented permanently on long or short-term leases? (Even if you're not domiciled in France for tax purposes you may be subject to French income tax on letting income and, on the positive side, if your *domicile fiscal* is in France your investment may qualify for tax relief. (See Chapter 15.) Or are you buying entirely for business purposes: relocating your office, creating *chambres d'hôtes* (bed and breakfast), an 'English' estate agency, a small hotel/restaurant . . .?

Your aims will directly affect your purchase, renovation and maintenance budgets.

Permanent residence implies the choice of quality and lasting materials you will find comfortable to live with, while a holiday-home purchase implies practical, easily maintained materials with a more limited life which can be replaced from time to time at reasonable cost.

If your property is planned to be a holiday home you may have to consider employing a local company for outside maintenance work. In wooded areas, *débroussaillage* (shrub and long grass clearance) of at least 50 metres around your property is obligatory as a precaution against forest fires. There is also an official obligation, every 10 years, to do up (*ravaler*) front, rear and side walls of apartment blocks *and* houses, which is strictly applied in the Paris area and by certain other municipalities throughout France.

PREMISES FOR RENTAL OR OTHER BUSINESS PURPOSES

Business taxation details are outside the scope of this book, but if you are seeking premises for rental or other business purposes the guidelines below will be useful:

◆ *Taxe professionnelle* (local business tax) applies to all lessors of furnished (*meublé*) accommodation unless you rent out part of your habitual (principal) residence *and* are also zero rated for income tax. Exemption also applies if you let out on a weekly basis (*à la semaine*) part of your principal *or* holiday (second) residence for not more than 12 weeks annually.

- If your annual rental income exceeds €23,000, or more than 50 per cent of your total annual income is rental, you will be considered to be a professional landlord. Registration *before* you go into business (when you will probably only have a first-year income forecast) with your local *Registre du Commerce* is obligatory: a chicken and egg situation. A *louer en meublé professionnel* or *LMP* (professional landlord of furnished accommodation) is, however, exempt from paying capital gains on any property which he resells at least five years after the date of purchase.

- If you are not considered to be a professional landlord you may be exempt from paying income tax on rental incomes from grant-holding students and people living on Social Security allowances.

- If you operate a business on a sole trader basis (*en nom propre*) using a room in your home as your day-time office, this should not affect the way the property is taxed as your private residence.

- Since the beginning of August 2003 new legislation regarding business activity (*Loi pour l'initiative économique 2003-72*) has made it easier to operate (*exercer*) and register (*domicilier*) many businesses from home addresses provided there are no regulations to the contrary in the general conditions which relate to your residence. For example, if you live in a residential apartment block there may be a prohibitive clause, even if you are a proprietor. **You are, therefore, advised to check the regulations prevailing at the time of purchase**, preferably using a bilingual taxation expert. They advertise regularly in property magazines such as *French Property News* (see Further Reading). Or, if your French is up to it, check directly, for free, with the local tax office (*hôtel/centre des impôts*). You will find their addresses under *impôts, trésor public* in the *Pages Jaunes* telephone directory (or use the www.pagesjaunes.fr website).

Useful vocabulary

acquéreur	buyer
agence immobilière	estate agency
architecte	architect
expert (estimation immobilière)	property valuer

géomètre expert	chartered surveyor
immobilier ancien	property over five years old
immobilier neuf	property under five years old
location meublé	furnished accommodation
louer en meublé professionnel	professional landlord of furnished accommodation
maître d'œuvre	(building) project manager (probably an architect)
résidence principale	main home
résidence secondaire	second home

2

Some Typical and Not So Typical Conversions, Renovations and Restorations

Perhaps you've decided what to buy and why, but are still looking, or perhaps you've found your dream property. Or maybe you're keeping your options open on both situation and type of property while you're scanning property details and advertisements to see what catches your interest.

Whatever your situation, this chapter will give you a glimpse of what can and has been done to various old properties in those areas of France, such as Britanny, Normandy, Savoy, Provence and Languedoc-Roussillon, which remain popular with British buyers. Reference is also made to the Dordogne and an exceptional Corsican tale is mentioned. We'll look at continuous improvements which become a way of life, an unending work of art, or something more practical with definite, or almost definite, start and finish dates. Bear in mind that local regulations may take precedence over national building regulations (see Chapter 5, page 44), and what you've seen and liked in Britanny, for example, will not necessarily be allowed in the neighbouring region (*région*) of Lower Normandy where you would prefer to live.

Figure 1   Brittany *longère*. Granite built with long slate roof and heavy granite arches or surrounds to windows.

BRITANNY

Case study – a *longère*

The classic rural property is the *longère*: as its name suggests, a long barn-type farmhouse. Our case study is of a late 17th century example in the Morbihan *département*, the southernmost part of the region: a granite-walled, slate-roofed building languishing in a garden which was wasting away.

Stabling, a cowshed, a clay-walled living room and a hayloft were transformed, after eight months of hard and continuous work, into a spacious habitation providing a lounge and separate dining room (leading into the kitchen), as well as four bedrooms for friends and family visits. All the load-bearing ceiling beams on the ground floor were stripped down, sanded and treated with fungicide. The downstairs arched windows overlooking the garden were restored, with their granite surrounds, to their original perfection. A chalk-based plaster for the interior walls replaced the original clay base, bringing light to what was formerly a sombre abode.

The dining room and lounge

Rooms have been laid out so that the dining room is entered directly from the front door, with the dining room table positioned to make the most of sunlight all year round. The hearth of the lounge fireplace, which is over 250 years old and made from granite blocks set into the wall, and the mantelpiece beam, support low rows of loosely laid stone slabs which retain the heat. This, in effect, was where the farmers cooked their meals.

Traditional style floor tiles which are regularly oiled for cleansing and preservation purposes have been laid onto a slightly raised floor. The original clay floor made no provision for damp-proofing so metal sheeting has been laid onto a sand base, covered with flexible plastic sheeting, to provide the base for this new floor.

The kitchen

Running on from the dining room, the kitchen has been ingeniously designed and fitted in keeping with the traditional old-world character of the house, while offering modern units. Floor to ceiling cupboards are given preference over wall elements, and wall tiling is limited. There are several high open shelves full of bric-a-brac, and the doors and facades of the floor storage units have a bright yellow lacquered finish. Near the window a breakfast bar doubles as a side-board in the evenings. The cooker is quite separate – not integrated with the tiled work tops. The overall effect is a harmonious and natural extension to the living areas of dining room and lounge.

The garden

As the property is a second home the owner has replanted some fruit, fir and oak trees and some hardy perennials, which flower from April to October, with an eye to easy maintenance. Hydrangea shrubs, in particular, thrive in the Britanny soil and climate. The meadow grass only needs occasional weeding, and some non-cemented shale paving stones, just simply laid down, are the garden paths.

Other properties

Renovations can, of course, take much longer than eight months. In this instance, the owner is Parisian and was no doubt on hand regularly to oversee the work and probably put in the finishing touches. This was not the case with a British couple living in London, who bought a similar property in Britanny in 1990 for £25,000 and spent around £80,000 and many holidays over 12 years doing it up. Re-wiring (see Chapter 9, page 101) and a leaking roof meant they couldn't actually live in the property for the first five years. Eventually a local architect was brought in to supervise a large part of the renovation. The property was valued at the end of 2002 at around £150,000 (approximately €225,000) – not too bad, after all.

Sizes of *longères* do, of course, vary: from a quite respectable 100 m² to a large property with about 400 m² floor area. A 400 m² *longère* in the north coast *département* of Côtes-d'Armor and requiring restoration had, for example, an asking price of €105,000 in 2002.

LOWER NORMANDY

Case study – a *pressoir*

In the heart of the Augeron cider and Camembert producing area, a former *pressoir* (cider press-house) now enjoys a residential life. The classic exterior still features oak half-timbered facades with intervening strips of clay-plastering. (If re-pointing of the joints between timbers and the plaster or stone parts of the walls is required, a limestone mortar is strongly recommended.) The ample interior floor area was ripe for numerous possibilities.

The new owners have sensibly maintained the original room structures and prolonged and overhanging sloping roofs, respecting the 18th century architectural style. This *queue de geai* ('jay's tail') roof offered storm

Figure 2   Normandy *pressoir*. Enlarged view of the overhanging *queue de geai* (jay's tail) roof and the *colombage* (half-timbered) walls with timbering partly over the windows.

protection when agricultural workers went up the outside staircase to the granary loft. An interior staircase has now replaced this staircase: safer and less of an invitation to possible intruders. Slate roof tiles have replaced the thatch, reducing maintenance costs and lowering the insurance premium.

The living room and sitting room

As with our *longère*, the beaten-earth floors have now been tiled. The entrance area and sitting room have diagonally laid patchworks of variously shaded terracotta tiles and the living room has authentic 18th century tiles which have been stripped down, oiled and then waxed. (Re-waxing, using a natural wax, is recommended every six months.)

The old mill-stone press room has been emptied of its cumbersome machinery to become the spacious lounge with oak-beamed ceilings. A specially commissioned stone fireplace, using local stone, with an oak mantelpiece, has been built by a local craftsman in the Norman tradition. A wide-spread wrought-iron chandelier gives the illusion of reducing the ceiling height to make the room feel cosier.

To brighten what is now the sitting room, the clay-filled parts of the *colombage* (half-timbered façades) have been stripped out and a large double-glazed plate-glass window has been installed *behind* the timberwork, which remains in its entirety. Architectural integrity is thus preserved while the owners enjoy a better view of the garden.

The kitchen

As a utility building the press-house had few windows. Like the dining room, the kitchen now benefits from a new window (a standard one, which opens and shuts for aeration purposes) with the *colombage* timberwork still in place. The cooker and dishwasher are housed in beech-stained kitchen units which blend in with the beams and tiles.

A special bedroom and bathroom

A separate outbuilding, amid fruit trees, has been converted to a guest room, and part of the *colombage* has been completely removed to house a plate-glass window with an entirely clear view. The exterior of the defunct brick bread oven in this room has been meticulously restored and guests can see it, or dream about it, from their bed. Yellow-painted ceiling beams offset the generally rustic décor.

In the main house a small bathroom has been fitted into a corner of one of the bedrooms and a sky-light situated over the wash basin provides all the natural light required. A wall mirror reflecting the outside timberwork offers a constant reminder of the property's character.

Care of old exterior timberwork is implicit in the choice of all *colombage* properties, and selection and application of suitable wood sealers should not be neglected (see advice given for preserving wooden shutters under 'Shutters' in Chapter 9 and also under 'General maintenance' in Chapter 13). As they are specialist properties, it is difficult to give guidance on asking prices for cider-press houses for restoration with residence in mind. Taking into account that most press machinery is securely fitted into place, the 'removal' cost should not be neglected. A gutted *pressoir* may be a more attractive proposition.

UPPER SAVOY

Case study – a chalet
Many old chalets were actually of stone construction not wood, but this particular one in the Mont Blanc area, once a huge farmhouse, is wood throughout in keeping with the traditional image people have of chalets. Originally in these chalets the largest rooms were the hay store and livestock shelters, while the farming family lived in rather poky rooms with small windows.

The interior has, therefore, been completely transformed and now provides wide views over the garden. And the new owners have managed to use timber reclaimed entirely from chalet ruins: authenticity assured.

The ground floor
The farmers' living quarters have been converted to three bedrooms, each with a bathroom.

Figure 3   Savoy wood chalet.

The large lounge, small sitting room, dining room, kitchen and master bedroom
These rooms occupy the first floor, which would have been the fodder store.
Wood is everywhere in the lounge and there is an imposing fireplace,
numerous windows and an open staircase and landing with decorative
woodwork, which is often found on the outside balconies of local
farmhouses. The more intimate sitting room with a lower ceiling features fir
wood floors and double-glazed fir wood windows.

With five bedrooms in all, a large fitted kitchen was necessary to cater for
everyone, and a brass and steel restaurant cooker, which tones in beautifully
with the natural woods, has been installed. Salernes tiles (see 'Wall tiles' in
Chapter 10 and under 'Private labels' in Chapter 14) have been laid on the
wall behind the cooker.

The dining room, on a split-level with the lounge and with the kitchen to the
side, is dominated by the main table, in fir wood, which seats 12, while a
huge floor-to-ceiling larch-wood dresser runs along one wall. The master

bedroom has a four-poster bed in the best local tradition and French
windows open onto the outside balcony.

Under the eaves

Sturdy beams follow the direction of the ceiling boards in the attic bedroom
while the wall boards, by way of contrast, run vertically (floor to ceiling)
avoiding all possibility of monotony. Even the pelmets and the bookshelf
above the bed are the result of elegant carpentry. The roof's double lining
guarantees insulation.

Throughout the chalet, old handmade Savoy furniture, in chestnut, fir, larch
and pine wood, is also a mark of careful restoration.

PROVENCE

Case study – a *mas* farmhouse

On the borders of the Bouches-du-Rhône and Vaucluse *départements*,
slightly further south than Peter Mayle country, an old Provençal *mas*
farmhouse has been resuscitated.

In addition to the thought given to the interior renovation, particular
attention has been paid to the position and design of the swimming pool and
to the creation of shaded, naturally ventilated, outside relaxation areas so
that the Mediterranean climate can be best appreciated.

The kitchen

Light concrete blocks (*béton cellulaire*), easy to use for the DIY person, form
the work-tops and open storage areas and traditional blue Catalan tiles
provide a covered work-top finish and wall protection above the cooker.
With the brushed steel cookers overhung by copper cooking pots, rustic
charm pervades a modern kitchen. Enamelled sandstone floor tiles studded
with small inset blue squares complete the blue décor.

Cane matting over a metal framework is the open air kitchen 'extension' for
al fresco meals. Provençal stone slabs form the patio floor.

Figure 4 Provençal *mas* farmhouse. South-facing façade, showing stonework and terrace. (That *is* a solid stone table!).

The lounge and dining room

A wide archway separates the dining room from the lounge, breaking up the rectangular symmetry. These rooms were created from the former barn area of the property. The new fireplace and the walls, ceiling beams and ceiling boards have all been painted with a distemper whitewash tinged with yellow ochre, giving a warm feeling and matt finish.

An attic bedroom and a retro style bathroom

The original attic roof tiles were removed, a heat reflecting screen laid down (it can get pretty warm at roof level down in the South), and then the tiles were replaced. Rockwool insulation slabs complete the roof insulation and the plasterboard ceiling finish leaves exposed ceiling beams.

On the first floor the retro bathroom boasts a Victorian-style pedestal cast-iron enamel bath unearthed in an antiques shop and the two pedestal mounted wash basins are 1920s replicas. The old parquet flooring was taken up and under-the-floor plumbing installed (to avoid pipes running round the room) before re-flooring with enamelled sandstone tiles. As it is a spacious room humidity is not a problem, and just the splash areas around the bath and wash basins have wall tiles.

The swimming pool and garden

Discreetly situated to one side of the house, the stone swimming pool (see 'Swimming pools' in Chapter 12) is surrounded by pot plants, like an ornamental pond. A tiled sloping roof overhang from the house offers a shaded terrace for lounging pool-watchers.

A small stone-floored patio, with a cane roof, like the kitchen 'extension', leads from the south-facing front of the house to the swimming pool area and an adjacent outbuilding has been fitted out with two guest bedrooms. Other parts of the garden are luxuriously planted and there are cherry trees and a superb ash tree. The under-soil automatic garden sprinkler system is a boon in the summer – May to September.

LANGUEDOC-ROUSSILLON

Case study – a *relais*

Just south of Narbonne, the area's capital in the Roman era, a local French couple have completely transformed a mid-17th century *relais* (coaching inn) as their own home and guesthouse.

Having originally bought and renovated part of the property 20 years ago, which became their home, the couple had the opportunity in the 1990s to buy the remaining buildings, which consisted of the stables, sheep shelter and hayloft. They needed extra income and after three years doing everything themselves in all their spare time they succeeded in creating a small guesthouse. This transformation is particularly interesting: not only were gravel, sand and stones extracted freely, if exhaustingly, from the countryside but reclaimed materials, such as wooden railway sleepers, have been used imaginatively. In this way the cost of restoration has been minimised.

Re-roofing (see 'Roofing' in Chapter 9) was the priority. Even the cool, thick stone walls were starting to buckle under the weight of the cement originally used to fix the roof tiles. So these tiles were de-cemented and refitted with modern-day glue.

Each room of the guesthouse was then created in turn, from top to bottom, rather than in general phases such as re-flooring followed by redecorating. Where possible, original fitments, such as cupboard and room doors, have been kept to preserve authenticity.

The dining room

This was formerly the stables, and the manger is still there as a show piece. Massive ceiling beams contrast with the restored, traditional striped ceiling of cross-planking and plaster strips. The original stable doors are now the dining room entrance.

The patio and winter-garden

The adjoining patio and winter-garden were the former sheep shelter (*bergerie*). A glass roof has replaced the original roof. This is where an open

Figure 5 (a) Languedoc-Roussillon *relais*. Entrance view. Note the stone walls and double-door stable doors (now the dining room entrance). (b) The side view of the *relais*, showing the gabled roof and three floors.

staircase using railway sleepers as steps and sporting home-made wrought-iron banisters and handrails leads upstairs.

The upstairs bedrooms

The two upstairs bedrooms, each sleeping four people, are decorated with a distemper mix of limestone, powdered milk and natural pigments. Part of the sloping roof of what was the hayloft has been justifiably sacrificed to provide space for an open terrace, with view of the surrounding vineyards. Access is from the larger bedroom.

Final note

Normally, major renovation work does not attract official subsidies if you're doing everything yourself, unless you're a professional builder by trade; but an exemption was made in this instance. Moreover, this *chambres d'hôtes* businesss is now booming all year round: a success story.

Other properties

Moving north-west about 200 miles to Eymet in the Dordogne (Bergérac area), an expatriate property developer has bought, from the municipality, what is left of the water-mill and has an ambitious hotel complex plan which will bring a lot of new tourist business to this already popular area. Having received municipal approval of the tasteful renovation to her own home in Eymet, a subsidy will probably be granted, but almost certainly not before work is well under way. (Eymet, incidentally, has an expatriate population of nearly 40 per cent.)

More conventionally, in the south-east 'Black Périgord' area of Dordogne an Anglo-American couple, moving from California, have bought a solid stone-built house. On much less than GCSE level French, they are dealing with local recommended builders, just one of whom they can really converse with (and only in English at the present). Although the house appears quite habitable in its present state, considerable modernisation is desired. A preliminary verbal estimate for the cost of the work is between €55,000 and €75,000. The stone terrace and its view actually clinched the sale (more about terraces in Chapter 12).

If awards existed for property renovation and there was a motivation and determination category, a German shepherd in southern Corsica would be a strong contender.

On a cycling holiday in Corsica 25 years ago, this young German tourist had his bike stolen and at the same time discovered a derelict shepherd's lodge and sheep shelter. He bought these buildings, slowly renovating them while building up his flock of sheep, which regularly produce prize-winning cheese. Mains electricity was only laid on just four years ago.

FINALLY

Details of cost, choosing and finding materials and ensuring that the property you are buying is in fact authentic – not just a clever replica – are dealt with in other chapters. Having plenty of time available and being on the spot before and during renovation are ideal.

Prices of properties for renovation vary considerably throughout France. Provence, for example, is more expensive than neighbouring Languedoc-Roussillon, although both enjoy the Mediterranean sun. Generally speaking, country properties are cheaper than suburban properties which, in turn, are cheaper than town centre properties. Any property with a good sea-view, or close to the sea, will be more valuable than comparable properties just a little inland.

Useful vocabulary

aggrandisement	extension
aménagé(e)/aménageable	converted/convertible
bastide	stone house (South of France)
bergerie	shepherd's lodge/sheep shelter
brocanteur	second-hand goods dealer
cabanon	country cottage or small house
cave/cave vôutée	cellar/vaulted cellar
chalet	chalet or cottage
chaumière	thatched cottage

colombage	half-timbered (mainly Normandy)
comble or *grenier*	loft or attic
écurie	stable
étable	cowshed
ferme	farm
hameau	hamlet
jumelé(e)	semi-detached
longère	long barn-style house (mainly Britanny)
maçonnerie	brick or stonework
maison de maître	period country house or mansion
maison de village	(old) village house
mansardé (étage/pièce)	attic (storey/room)
mas	Mediterranean farmhouse
moulin	mill
piscine	swimming pool
plafond	ceiling
plain-pied	one level (single storey)
plan d'eau	lake
poutre/poutrelle	beam
rénové(e)	renovated
restauré(e)	restored
sous-sol	basement
toiture	roof

3

Location, Position and Outlook

You may at this stage have a much clearer idea of what and why you want to buy, but unless you're being posted to Bordeaux, Geneva (it's cheaper to live on the French side of the Franco-Swiss border), Grenoble, Lille, Lyons, Marseilles, Montpellier, Nice, Paris, Toulouse or elsewhere in France for five years as part of a structured international career with a multinational, where to buy may still be a nice problem.

FACTORS TO CONSIDER

Are you looking for easy access to the local village or town, hospitals and other amenities? Or are you seeking complete seclusion and are prepared to cope with the rigours of a rude winter climate in hilly and mountainous areas which may leave country and secondary roads in a less than perfect state for a good part of the year? The extent and condition of the motorway (*autoroute*) network, national trunk (*RN*) roads and main departmental (*départementale*) D roads throughout France are second to none. Other roads are maintained by the local community and road maintenance funds and the state of the roads can vary enormously.

If you're buying a main home to be lived in all year round, take into account heavy tourist influx in seasonal periods, and traffic bottle-neck areas (the motorway running through Lyons is bumper-to-bumper whenever there are short and long holiday periods) which, with the suggested diversions, can transform otherwise peaceful environments. France is the number one tourist destination in the world, and, after Paris, Provence, the Côte d'Azur and the French Alps are the leading touristy areas. Lyons is the gateway town, by road, from the north, east and west of France.

Even if planning permission (see Chapter 5) authorises the construction, conversion or extension work you envisage, will you ruin the armchair view you enjoy over your Atlantic or Mediterranean coastline or over your neighbour's rolling meadows? Many old farmhouses or special purpose dwellings had ground floors which served as sheep or cattle sheds or for other utilitarian purposes, where the surrounding view was not a consideration. Are the front and rear main walls facing the best direction as regards outlook and sunny aspect or would prohibitive transformation or reconstruction costs be involved to put matters right? Will modifying a solid stone wall, over 200 years old, make it more or less sound, more or less wind- or rain-proof? Restoration, preserving the good elements, rather than renovation, in this instance would be wiser.

If holiday lets are going to provide part of your income on a professional basis and you're living on the spot, consider, perhaps, an area that has steady business throughout the year rather than overwhelming peak periods.

TYPICAL PROPERTIES IN DIFFERENT REGIONS

Maisons de maître, *maisons de village* and *fermettes*, ripe for renovation, are found throughout France, reflecting regional differences in style and construction. High sloping roofs in areas such as Normandy, Britanny and Centre (the Loire Valley) are suitable for dormer windows while lower sloping roofs, particularly in Provence, are ideal for velux windows. Red-brick exterior walls are prevalent in the northern regions while thick stone exterior walls have no particular geographical boundaries. Property prices, of course, vary from region to region, with the Paris and Cannes areas at the top of the league, followed by the rest of the Côte d'Azur and the prestigious areas of the French Alps.

Below are translated extracts from advertisements in the July-August 2003 issue of *L'Immobilier des Notaires* magazine. This magazine carries property advertisements on behalf of notaries who also act as estate agents. These extracts, with my comments in brackets, give an indication of types of property, with prices, for renovation in some areas of France. In some instances rough comparisons can be made between similar properties in different areas, although individual property sizes, plot sizes and the condition of the buildings vary, preventing strict comparisons.

Top prices

Paris (11th arrondissement). Self-contained house with gd. floor + 3 storeys (each around 26 m^2). Four two-roomed units for investment possible. €442,000.

Pays de la Loire region (the west coast). Large country property requiring restoration. Large attic. Spacious outbuildings. Around two hectares of land. Open to offers (but no doubt at least €400,000 is sought).

Properties offering numerous possibilities

Centre region (the Loire Valley). Habitable house requiring renovation. Loft. Other buildings used as a barn, stable and cowshed, with two rooms above. €72,019.

Franche-Comté region (the Jura mountains, near the Swiss border). For investors. Large house with five main rooms in first class order. Conversion possibilities for separate four-room area and possibly a studio apartment. 15 acres of land. €225,000.

Britanny. In need of renovation: two-floor *longère* stone building with slate roof. Extremely large living area potential. 453 m² plot. (No price given, small plot.)

Britanny. Stone-built house requiring renovation, with ruins. Large garden. €142,500. (Are you paying for the ruins? If so, what is their historical interest? Do you need them?)

Farm buildings (*corps de ferme*), more than a *fermette*

Auvergne region, Cantal *département* (one of the cheapest property areas in France). Stone farm buildings for renovation. Main house, stable, lean-to barn and other outbuildings. Just over one acre of land. €76,000.

Vendée. (Coastal *département* of the Pays de la Loire region). Farm buildings for renovation. Main house, convertible 35 m² attic, two barns, stable and large shed. €118,974.

Atlantic coast *départements* – holiday/letting property and an unfinished property

Loire-Atlantique. 52 m² (that's small) bungalow, no garage or garden. Ideal for lets. Some work required. €50,800.

And further down this coast:

Charente-Maritime. Near the sea, 82 m² house with two upstairs bedrooms and bathroom. Lounge (perhaps an extension?) needs to be completed as does the shower room. Separate dining room. New roof, including the framework. Small garden. Some work required. €111,175. inclusive of all fees. (What's the construction story here? And does 'inclusive of all fees' mean that both notary charges and their fee as estate agents are included in the price? A *prix, acte en main* final completion price would be clearer.)

Various properties in the Centre region (Loire Valley)

Loir-et-Cher *département*. 90 mins. from Paris. Small farm in need of restoration. Two buildings, one of which is under restoration and has a

WC and laundry room, with possibilities for three rooms and a mezzanine. The other building has a large lounge and kitchen area. One acre of land. €59,500. (If restoration is required, where and when does the 'under restoration' work stop?).

Loir-et-Cher *département.* Town centre. Typical 16th century house with restoration requiring completion. (So it's no longer *under* restoration.) Ground and upstairs floor with further floor housing a converted loft. 27 m² lounge, three/four bedrooms. Mains drainage. €84,457. (Sounds interesting, subject to a professional survey.)

Loiret *département.* Two (detached) barn buildings with residential conversion possibilities, one of which serves as a garage, stables and barn with overhead granary/loft area. €95,572.

Useful vocabulary

acte (authentique) en main	with possession of property completion deed
à finir	(building/renovation work) to be completed
amenagé	converted or fitted out
corps de ferme	(main) farm buildings
en cours de restauration	restoration in progress
prix à discuter	price negotiable
quelques travaux à prévoir	some (building/renovation) work will be necessary
tous frais compris	inclusive of all charges or fees

4

Estate Agents, Visiting Properties and the Buying Procedure

This chapter is in three sections. The first considers effective methods of **property prospecting** from the UK, including use of the Internet. The second looks at **visits**, and questions you should, and in some instances, must ask construction and property valuation experts, estate agents or notaries, the seller (*le vendeur*), the *service de cadastre* (municipal land registry department), etc. Estate agents and notaries, for example, are of course legally bound to give you certain information, but other information, such as wind and rain frequency in the locality, will only be forthcoming if *you* think of asking the question. If you're looking at properties in the normally sunny Midi on a dull day, ask yourself if the living rooms are facing south, south-east or south-west. If you're visiting in the school holidays, will you welcome the noise from the nearby school in term-time? The third section covers the **buying** procedure and what the official documents mean: you may well not be buying through a bilingual agent, or you may be dealing directly, *particulier à particulier*, with the owner before you sign the *compromis de vente*.

PROPERTY PROSPECTING

Considerable initial 'prospecting' can be accomplished from your UK home by studying the property pages and advertisements in the quality Sunday papers and subscribing to French property magazines.

ENGLISH-LANGUAGE PROPERTY MAGAZINES

The main English property magazines are *French Property News*, published monthly by French Property News, 6 Burgess Mews, Wimbledon, London SW19 1UF (annual subscription £18) and *Focus on France*, published every two months by Outbound Publishing, 1 Commercial Road, Eastbourne, East Sussex BN21 3XQ (annual subscription £13.50). Both magazines have lively, informative articles, which sometimes include renovation case histories, and carry plenty of colour advertisements. Their respective websites are www.french-property-news.com and www.worldofpropertyexhibition.com.

If you are particularly interested in south-west France, including the Dordogne and Lot-et-Garonne *départements* and the Limousin region, the English-language monthly newspaper *The News* has property and building services advertisements and articles. Its address is SARL Brussac, 225 route d'Angoulême, 24000 Périgueux, France. Subscription enquiries can be emailed to subs@french-news.com.

One big advantage of dealing with 'English' estate agents, who advertise in these publications, is that they often specialise in properties for renovation, as an important part of their English market, and will also have a better understanding of English attitudes and desires than their French colleagues.

FRENCH PROPERTY MAGAZINES AND WEBSITES

If you wish to subscribe to the French magazine *L'Immobilier des Notaires* the annual subscription, for 10 issues, is €41.60. Your subscription order (*abonnement*) and remittance or credit card details with expiry date should be sent to EXEDIM, BP 21, 19231 Pompadour, France. The website address is www.immonot.com and you can look up the property descriptions, which regrettably are only available in French, following the instructions in English. The colour photos can, however, be enlarged on screen.

Unlike estate agents, who are free to fix their own fees, notaries throughout France have to respect standard sliding scale negotiation fees on property sales. (See 'Visiting' in this chapter.) Notaries sometimes advertise a property with the price *acte en main*: the total price, inclusive of presentation and negotiation fees (commission), registration fees and search and conveyance fees. (See 'Notary charges' at the end of this chapter.)

One of the largest chains of estate agents in France is ORPI, who have offices in almost every *département*. The website www.orpi.com has particularly good English descriptions of properties with the usual possibility of enlarging the colour photos. The ORPI French monthly printed magazine, *100% exclusivités ORPI mag*, costing €2.50 and only sold in France, contains several thousand property advertisements, with many in colour, for which its branches are sole agents. ORPI agents will accompany potential buyers to builders for work estimates if they (ORPI) have sole agency rights.

The two main French magazines with a selection of estate agents' colour advertisements are *Logic-Immo*, published every three weeks, and *Mag Immo*, published fortnightly. Between them they cover most of France with regional and *départementales* editions. You can subscribe to *Mag Immo*, and see their geographical coverage, via their website www.h3sgroup.com (only in French). A minimum of three months for any one edition, i.e. six issues, costs €24; not too cheap if you need several areas and a long period. The *Logic-Immo* minimum subscription period is six months, which costs €18, i.e. for eight issues of any one edition. It's cheaper than its competitor, normally has more pages, and with 46 geographical editions has wider coverage of France. The website www.logic-immo.com is not in English, but there are some property photos, and you must click on '*nos éditions*' to see the individual edition areas. Then write, enclosing your cheque in euros, to

CMM/LOGIC-IMMO, 444, rue Paradis, 13008 Marseille, France. A little cumbersome.

Most of the above-mentioned websites have facilities for registering online, with your email address, your specific interest and for punching in your immediate search, while you remain connected to see what comes up. It should also be borne in mind that both *Mag Immo* and *Logic-Immo* magazines are available free from countless bakers, small stores and petrol stations if you're in France.

See Useful Websites on page 172 for other property search websites.

FRENCH PROPERTY SHOWS IN THE UK

Still in the UK, the two leading French property shows are:

◆ The French Property Exhibition, at Olympia, London in January each year, run by *French Property News.* Tel: (UK) 020 8543 3113, email: info@french-propertynews.com

◆ Focus on France Property Show (part of the World of Property Exhibition), at Sandown Park Racecourse in March each year, run by Outbound Publishing. Tel: (UK) 01323 726040, website: www.worldofpropertyexhibition.com.

These are ideal venues to meet estate agents specialising in France and/or the UK office or partner of the estate agency, or perhaps the French agent, that you have already contacted. Exchange ideas, compare areas, look at the reality of the market, modify your thoughts, be more precise . . .

Useful vocabulary	
abonnement	subscription (magazine, etc.)
acte en main	possession of (property) completion deed
particulier à particulier	directly between seller and buyer
service de cadastre	municipal land registry department
vendeur	seller

VISITING PROPERTIES

You are now in France, having fixed appointments – either in the same area to see and compare different properties, or in different areas to compare environments and ambiance and see what you get for the same budget. At least two weeks, especially if it's your first house-hunting trip to France, would be ideal. Hire a car, if you've flown over, and you're comparing *départements* and areas.

Signing a *bon de visite*

Estate agents in general will be keen to drive you to visits and show you properties. They are unlikely to give you the keys to properties, even if they are unoccupied, and jealously guard addresses of properties (*biens*) on their books if they don't have the sole agency. You will quite possibly be asked to sign a *bon de visite* (see opposite) **before** your visit. This certifies the date of your visit and briefly describes the property giving its address. There will usually be a clause indicating that you will not sign an agreement to purchase the property directly with the seller (*vendeur*) or through another agent/notary within a 12-month period. The legal weight of the *bon de visite* is debatable, but its *raison d'être* is understandable. If you're interested in a property you have visited and find it is cheaper in another estate agency, go back to the first agent and negotiate.

Property descriptions

Property description sheets (*fiches techniques*), with the exception of elaborate brochures for luxurious *demeures* and *châteaux*, are notoriously light on information.

French logic often means that descriptions are laid out on a grid system with the number of main rooms, which excludes kitchens and all utility rooms, counted in terms of Fs or Ts. A *villa type F4* indicates a house with four main rooms, apart from the kitchen. The number of bedrooms will be further down the description sheet.

You should familiarise yourself with the metric system of room surface areas as opposed to room dimensions. A *salon-salle à manger de 30 m²*, for example, is a reasonable size for a through lounge/dining room. Bedrooms

---

BON DE VISITE

Paris, le (date)

Monsieur et/ou Madame

Demeurant à (your address) . . . .

. . . .

. . . .

déclare(nt) avoir visité ce jour

UNE MAISON

UN APPARTEMENT

UN LOCAL COMMERCIAL

sis(e) à

---

smaller than 9 m^2 are approaching box rooms. A total habitable floor area (*surface habitable*) of 100 m^2 is a reasonable size for a three-bedroom house, with separate kitchen, dining room, lounge, bathroom and WC. Below that would be small. A garage (*non-habitable*) of 15 m^2 is a standard size.

If you are buying an apartment, and in some instances houses on estates, the notion of exact measurement of the *surface habitable* may affect price. The *Loi Carrez* (Carrez's Law) for properties concerned stipulates that habitable room surface areas must be shown on all official property documents and be correct to within 5 per cent. If your surveyor, or you for that matter, prove that '85 m^2' is actually 80 m^2 you are in a strong position to get the price down before purchase. If you discover inaccurate measurements within one year of completion you are entitled to a pro-rata rebate on the purchase price. Cellars, garages and converted attics (with a room height of under 1.80 m) are not *surfaces habitables*.

Estate agents
The activity in an estate agent's showroom is not necessarily a guide to the agents' or their consultants' effectiveness, but an attractive window, kept up

to date with good colour photos, augurs well. A large part of estate agency work in France, in an extremely competitive market, is actively prospecting for additional properties for the agency's portfolio and this means that some offices look empty for a good part of the day. A properly organised staff roster will ensure there is always an experienced person in the office, unless it's a one-man-band. Some one-man-bands operate quite effectively from first floor offices, with or without a ground level outside display case or window, or even from home. Don't be put off by this. They often specialise in certain types of properties, e.g. cottages and farmhouses with outbuildings, or concentrate on business premises (*locaux commerciaux*).

Most agents dealing with an international clientele now have websites. The better websites have virtual reality images (360° views of interiors and exteriors) and this is where an awful lot of time can be saved for everyone concerned by avoiding unnecessary visits. National chains such as ORPI, Century 21, ERA and La Fôret have the resources to do this extremely well and of course offer the large-scale advantages of pooling all their property information.

Points to check
Before making an offer you should check the following points:

◆ Is the accurate plot size given? If not, see the *service de cadastre* at the town hall. It is not your responsibility to employ a surveyor to verify the plot size. Bear in mind, for example, if you want to build a 10x5 m swimming pool, which is a good standard size, you will need around twice that area free from garden greenery. (See Chapter 12.)

◆ Will you be allowed to extend, convert or re-build parts of the property? If your property is in a residential estate, check **first** any *lotissement* (housing estate) regulations (*cahier des charges*) with the agent or seller. You may be entitled to demolish part of the property, but not necessarily to re-build on the same piece of land. Is the building surface area on the plot at its limit, preventing any extension possibility?

◆ What has the municipality decided in terms of planning density permitted on your plot of land? Refer to the *service cadastre* for your plot reference.

The planning density (*coefficient d'occupation des sols* or *COS*) is fixed by the local town planning regulations (*PLU* or *POS*). Then look at the planning permission needed depending on the work envisaged (see Chapter 5).

◆ Are there any rights of way (*servitudes de passage*) through the property's land? How much is the land tax (*taxe foncière*) and the community tax (*taxe d'habitation*)? Bear in mind that alterations which increase the *surface habitable* will increase the community tax.

◆ If you plan to convert a former hayloft in a barn, or an attic in a house, to a habitable room, are the foundations adequate? Call in your architect or construction expert. Is your secluded or isolated property, which may have been built a century ago, now in an official *zone à risque* – flooding or forest fire risk area? Check with the town hall and ask around.

◆ Is the property in a termite risk area? There are over 3,000 municipalities with some infestation problem in more than half the French *départements*. The onus is on the seller, in these municipalities, to certify the situation.

◆ Is the property asbestos free? The onus is on the sellers of all houses, with building permits issued before 1 July 1997, to certify the situation.

◆ Is the property free of lead-content paints in officially declared risk municipalities? Officially declared risk areas include the Ile-de-France (Paris area). The onus is on the seller in these areas to certify the situation for houses (and apartments) built before 1948.

◆ Is the building as old as the seller claims? If you are buying a period property it is worth employing an *expert* to certify authenticity, although you may not obtain the exact date of construction, and also to give you an official valuation. If part of the property is advertised as having been renovated within the last 10 years, obtain the invoices for the work carried out. All structural work by an approved builder, properly insured, will have a 10-year guarantee (*garantie décennale*).

◆ Are the walls sound? Strips of wood-panelling (*lambris*) or chipboard or multiply wood-effect wall panelling may disguise damaged walls. They should be checked by your *expert*, especially if there appears to be an excessive amount or if they look out of place in the property.

- Is any construction work likely to be carried out in the area? Ensure that all future urban planning projects that could affect your property or plot are described on all official papers. The onus is on the seller to inform you if a public road is going to trim a slice off your front garden in two or three years' time.

- What about water supply and drainage? If the property you are buying has never been habitable – e.g. barns or outbuildings on farmland – and you are converting for residential use, consider the cost and practicability of linking up to mains drainage (*tout à l'égout*) or installing your own water purification system with septic tank (*fosse septique*). One or other is obligatory even if you have your own well for drinking water.

Estate agents' fees

Estate agents' fees are not standard, but they must be visibly displayed in their offices. Fees are usually between five and ten per cent on a sliding scale, with the most expensive properties subject to the lowest commission rate. The advertised price will normally include the agent's commission. You can therefore calculate the net selling price for the seller (*prix net vendeur*). It is possible, if the seller won't reduce their net price any further, that an estate agent will reduce their commission in the interests of a quick sale. If you do offer the full price advertised by an estate agent the seller is bound to accept your offer, because they will have signed a sales mandate (*mandat de vente*) to this effect with the estate agent. Gazumping cannot happen.

In some areas in France now, in common with many other EU countries, the seller pays the agent's commission. No doubt, you (the buyer) will in effect still be paying it as it will probably be 'included' in the advertised price.

Notaries' fees

The notary's negotiating fees (*honoraires de négociation*), which are incorporated in their advertised price for the property (unless otherwise indicated), are standard throughout France. They are:

Price portion up to €45,734.71: 5.0%, exclusive of VAT (*hors TVA* or *HT*)
Price portion above €45,734.71: 2.5%, exclusive of VAT
Plus 19.6% VAT

For example, for a property for which the seller has signed a sales mandate authorising the notary to sell the property for €76,224.51 (*prix net vendeur*) exclusive of negotiating fees, the VAT inclusive (*TTC*) negotiating fees would be:

Price portion up to €45,734.71 . . . . €2,734.94
Price portion from €45,734.71 to €76,224.51 . . . . €911.65
Total €3,646.59

As the purchaser, you pay the *net vendeur* price and the *honoraires de négociation* to the notary, who will extract these *honoraires* before remitting the balance to the seller, **plus** you also pay the notary fees (see final section of this chapter) for registration, search and conveyance work.

Assuming you have the choice for the property you've decided to buy, using a notary as intermediary offers certain advantages. The whole buying process should be quicker, if that's what you want; you can calculate the total buying cost more easily and you are almost guaranteed of dealing with a competent and scrupulous professional. Access to the notary profession is much stricter than to estate agency work, despite the code of practice laid down by the FNAIM (National Federation of Estate Agents), membership of which is optional.

PROPERTY AUCTIONS

House auctions (*maisons vendues aux enchères*) are ideal sources for obtaining properties suitable for renovation at knock-down prices. Auctions are announced well in advance in the local newspapers or, perhaps, in *L'Immobilier des Notaires* and give essential property details, including the exact land registry (*cadastre*) reference, a viewing date (you might want to bring your *architecte*) and the opportunity to study the local regulations (*cahier des charges*) if the property is in a private housing estate (*lotissement*).

You will need to deposit, before the auction commences, a certified cheque (returnable) representing 15 to 20 per cent of the reserve price so that your participation becomes official. The exact percentage depends on whether the auction is a *vente judiciaire* or *vente par adjudication devant notaire*. For *ventes judiciaires*, bids must be made through a barrister (*avocat*) attached to the tribunal concerned. In insolvency cases, *ventes judiciaires*, the reserve price is fixed by the creditor. The *vente par adjudication* reserve price is established by the notary and the seller and often represents the market valuation less 35 per cent.

As you are seeking to renovate you will not normally be buying from a *marchand de bien*, whose business is to buy old properties, renovate them to a liveable standard and sell them. They are property dealers and not estate agents. They are not even property speculators, as they will know the local market. They may, of course, compete with you in the auction. If you are considering the purchase of a property that was previously renovated some years before by a *marchand de bien*, and which now requires further renovation, bear in mind that while the actual work carried out was no doubt done by qualified professionals, the materials used would most probably not have been of the best quality. Don't necessarily use the same materials.

PRIVATE SALES

If you feel competent and confident enough to reply to sellers' advertisements directly, where no estate agent or notary is involved in the negotiating stage as an intermediary, there are several property advertisement magazines published, usually weekly, which only have private advertisements. Over 50 per cent of property sales in France are sold in this way, *particulier à particulier*.

These magazines cost between €2 and €3 from newsagents and kiosks. Many of the advertisements are accompanied by black-and-white or colour photos: *Le Journal des Particuliers* has *only* colour photos. The website for the *De Particulier à Particulier* magazine at www.pap.fr has particularly good English descriptions with colour photos that can be enlarged on screen and, for some properties, viewed through 360° as if you were there.

Useful vocabulary

avocat	barrister
biens	properties
bon de visite	visit certificate
cahier des charges	(estate) regulations or requirements
coefficient d'occupation des sols: COS	town planning density
fiche technique	(property) description sheet
fosse septique	septic tank
honoraires de négociation	notary's negotiating fees
locaux commerciaux	business premises
lotissement	residential estate
mandat de vente	sales mandate
maisons vendues aux enchères	house auctions
marchand de bien	property dealer
prix net vendeur	net sales price for the seller
PLU or *POS*	local town planning regulations
salon-salle à manger	through lounge-dining room
servitudes de passage	rights of way
surface habitable	habitable floor area
taxe d'habitation	community tax
taxe foncière	building and land tax
tout à l'égout	mains drainage
vente judiciaire	court order auction
vente par adjudication	sale by auction
zone à risque	(fire, flooding or other) risk area – planning permission is no longer granted

BUYING YOUR PROPERTY

Your written offer (*offre d'achat*) has been officially accepted. Or perhaps you've made up your mind following a final visit, and you, the seller and the estate agent are verbally in agreement on the price.

The next step is the *promesse de vente*, which may be a *compromis de vente* (preliminary contract of sale) or a *promesse unilatérale de vente* (unilateral agreement to sell). The principal distinction between the two is that the *compromis* is a commitment by both seller and buyer, while the *promesse unilatérale* engages only the seller. At this point, unless your French is fluent, you should ensure that the contract or agreement is written in French and English. If this is not possible, employ or consult a professional bilingual person.

While it is not in fact an obligation for your deposit to be held in a sequestered 'frozen' account, **it is strongly recommended. The promesse de vente should only be handled by an estate agent** (if a notary is not involved at this point) **whose headed paper certifies that they have professional financial liability insurance for at least €114,000**. The certification should read along the following lines:

'L'agence immobilière . . . . . . titulaire de la carte professionnelle Transactions sur immeubles, maisons et Fonds de Commerce délivrée sous le No . . . . . . par la Préfecture du . . . . . . et garantie par la . . . . . . (estate agents' federation, such as the FNAIM) pour un montant de €114,000.'

Compromis de vente
Essential clauses are:

◆ The description and precise address of the property

◆ Its total habitable area which is mandatory for apartments and houses subject to the *Loi Carrez* (see page 33)

◆ The agreed price and the amount of the agent's commission

◆ Completion and possession dates.

A *conditions suspensives* clause should also be included. This allows you, the buyer, to withdraw, recuperating your deposit (up to 10 per cent of the agreed price), if the loan you require for the purchase is not granted or if a town planning decision is revealed which will depreciate the value of the property (e.g. a rubbish tip is going to be built next door!). A *droit de préemption* clause ensures in the event of a compulsory purchase order before completion that the buyer recuperates their deposit.

Promesse unilatérale de vente

The seller agrees to reserve the property for the buyer at an agreed price for a specified and limited period of time. This contract should include the same clauses as in a *compromis de vente*.

While the buyer is not committed to purchase you still have to pay a deposit, which is normally 10 per cent of the price agreed by the seller. The deposit should be held in a sequestered account. There is no real reason, therefore, for choosing this unilateral agreement in preference to the *compromis* which binds both buyer and seller.

If you are buying *particulier à particulier* **you are advised to have the compromis de vente or option/promesse unilatérale de vente drawn up and signed before a notary**, preferably the notary who will draw up the *acte de vente definitive* (property completion deed). The notary will place your deposit in a sequestered account.

The completion date, which is usually within three months, will also have been stipulated, by mutual agreement, in the *promesse de vente*.

Cooling-off period

NB. A seven-day cooling-off period is now in force, during which the buyer can change their mind (no questions asked) regardless of whether a *promesse unilatérale* has been signed by the seller or a *compromis* signed by both buyer and seller. The seven-day period starts the day after first presentation (*première présentation*) of the agreement by registered post or messenger delivery. The buyer's deposit is returned entirely if they decide to withdraw. If either of these agreements has been drawn up by a notary the prospective buyer will often be asked to sign the *compromis* after the seven-day period has elapsed.

The notary's tasks

Notarial activity begins after the preliminary agreement: principally checking title and possible family/hereditary claims; asbestos, termite and lead-free paint certificates (see Chapter 9); outstanding loans or charges on the property; the *cadastre* registration of the property and town planning regulations.

The same notary acts for buyer and seller and is customarily chosen by the seller.

Acte de vente définitive

This reconfirms the information in the *promesse de vente* excluding now the *clauses suspensives*. A more detailed description of the property and land is given and planning regulations, certificates (see above) and ownership history going back at least 30 years are provided.

Notary charges (frais de notaire)

These are composed of *droits d'enregistrement et taxes* (council, departmental and regional taxes, stamp duty and land registration fee) paid to the state and the *émoluments de notaire* (notary's fees).

Droits d'enregistrement et taxes

These apply to all *ancien* properties, i.e. over five years old. The departmental and regional tax percentages levied on the sale price may vary slightly from area to area and have changed over the last 10 years, following the economic policies of local and regional governments in relation to the property market. In 2003 the average total of taxes, duty and land registration fee amounted to five to six per cent of the purchase price.

For the *neuf*, i.e. properties under five years old (which probably won't concern you), there are no council, departmental and regional taxes to be paid on purchase.

Emoluments de notaire

Do not confuse these with notary commission (*honoraires de négociation*).

There is a rather complicated sliding scale applying a percentage of the sale price of the property, which is the subject of the *acte authentique* prepared and drawn up by the notary. The notary will give you a provisional figure on request. You can also consult the English section of the www.immonot.com website (click on 'Conveyancing'), which will give you estimated figures enabling you to calculate approximate *émoluments*, including professional expenses.

For example, a property sold for €100,000 will incur *émoluments*, including professional expenses, of around €1,420;
a property sold for €200,000 will incur *émoluments*, including professional expenses, of around €2,620.

Useful vocabulary

acte authentique	property completion deed
compromis de vente	preliminary contract of sale
conditions suspensives	suspensive conditions
droits d'enregistrement et taxes	property purchase duty, taxes and registration fees
émoluments de notaire	notary professional fees
offre d'achat	formal purchase offer
promesse unilatérale de vente	unilateral (preliminary) agreement to sell

5

Understanding the Regulations

Nearly all exterior alterations to a property require planning permission (*permis de construire*) or official notification (*déclaration de travaux*) of the work intended and lodged at least one month in advance with your town hall **before** any work can start.

LOCAL REGULATIONS

If your property is in an estate (*lotissement*) you must first of all check the estate's rules and regulations (*cahier des charges*). These may vary enormously between *lotissements*. Apart from physical limits to the extent of work authorised, architectural styles, building materials used and outside colours can all be subject to strict rules. These regulations may be more restrictive than those of the municipality, which will in any case stipulate the maximum building surface permitted (*COS*) for your plot of land and any general regional rules concerning style, architecture and colours. The *cahier des charges* in private estates ceases to apply, however, after 10 years unless the owners' association – *syndic* or *association de copropriétaires* – votes to continue it, and the planning regulations then applicable are those of the municipality. The architects, town planning and environmental advisory council (*Conseil d'Architecture, d'Urbanisme et de l'Environment* or *CAUE*) for your *département* will also advise you. Look under *Architectes et agrées en architecture* in the *Pages Jaunes*.

NATIONAL REGULATIONS

The town planning regulations applicable throughout France (*Code de l'Urbanisme* or *CLU*), with floor or ground surface areas expressed in m^2 (square metres) and heights expressed in m (metres) are:

Conversions

All **conversion** projects, whether or not an extension is involved, from non-habitable to habitable floor surfaces (*surfaces habitables*) of over 170 m^2, must be accompanied by an architect's plans. This applies if you are converting, for example, a 170 m^2 + floor area barn to a house.

Extensions over 20 m^2

Permis de construire required. Application must be accompanied by an architect's plans if the total new floor surface (existing plus extension proposed) exceeds 170 m^2.

Extensions of 20 m^2 and under

Déclaration de travaux required, if the purpose, i.e. non-habitable, residential or business, of the property remains unchanged. Bear in mind that the extended property must respect the minimum distance limits from the next-door property or property boundaries if you're not semi-detached or terraced.

Additional storeys or roof heightening over 20 m^2

Permis de construire required.

Additional storeys or roof heightening under 20 m²
Déclaration de travaux required.

*Facades and side walls facelift (***ravalement***)*
Déclaration de travaux required. The original appearance must be retained.

Terraces	**Ground floor level**	
	Over 0.6 m high	*Déclaration de travaux* required.
	0.6 m high and less	No requirements.
	Upper floor level	
	Over 20 m²	*Permis de construire* required.
	20 m² and under	*Déclaration de travaux* required.
Verandas	Over 20 m²	*Permis de construire* required.
	20 m² and under	*Déclaration de travaux* required.
Windows	Identical replacement	No requirements.
	Additional or larger window	*Déclaration de travaux* required.

This means that installation of a velux window is the only item requiring *déclaration de travaux* if you are converting an attic area with a ceiling height of under 1.80 m, i.e. not *surface habitable*.

Stone or brick barbecues	2 m² and above or over 1.50 m high	*Déclaration de travaux* required.
	Under 2 m² and under, or 1.50 m high	No requirements.
Roof tiles	Identical replacements	No requirements.
	Different type of tile	*Déclaration de travaux* required.
Garden shed	**On land with no other building**	
	2 m² and above or over 1.50 m high	*Permis de construire* required.

	Under 2 m² and under, or 1.50 m high	No requirements.
	On land with a building	
	Under 2 m² and under, or 1.50 m high	No requirements.
	20 m² or under	*Déclaration de travaux* required.
	Above 20 m²	*Permis de construire* required.
Swimming pools	**Open**	*Déclaration de travaux* required.
	Covered, on land with a building	
	20 m² or under	*Déclaration de travaux* required.
	Over 20 m²	*Permis de construire* required.

Only permanent constructions are regulated. See Chapter 12 for safety measures.

Garages	**On land with no other building**	*Permis de construire* required.
	On land with an existing building	
	20 m² or under	*Déclaration de travaux* required.
	Over 20 m²	*Permis de construire* required.
Floors	Repairs/rebuilding/ renovation	No requirements.
Loggia	Window or wall enclosure	*Déclaration de travaux* required.
Boundary walls and fencing	Permanent construction	*Déclaration de travaux* required.

A *permis de construire* is necessary for any conversion that changes the use of a building or part of a building – e.g. a garage – to a small apartment.

PLANNING PERMISSION

Official application forms for the *permis de construire* are available from the town hall or from DDE (*Direction Départementale de L'Equipement*) offices. You, your appointed representative or other person who has an entitlement to carry out work on your property must lodge the application (four copies – we're in France, after all!) along with plans of the project and photos of the property as it is currently at the town hall. Ask for a receipt or send by registered post. After two weeks you should receive a letter giving you the date your application was officially received and a reference number as well as an indication of when a decision will be taken: normally, two months. If you have received no decision after two months, write asking for written confirmation that you are authorised to start work.

If you have bought a listed property **any** construction or alteration project, normally subject to a *permis de construire* or *déclaration de travaux*, will be submitted to specially appointed conservation architects for approval – or non-approval. The decision will almost certainly take longer than two months. Similarly, if you're thinking of buying a hotel or restaurant in a nature reserve park (*parc naturel*) only alterations which are considered as improvements for the well-being of your clientele will be considered.

You must always inform the town hall when work starts and finishes and you must have an outside noticeboard giving the property owner's name (you) and the work being carried out. There is a fine of €1,500 if this is not displayed. Don't forget to ask for a *certificat de conformité* (completed work approval certificate) within 30 days of finishing.

The *permis de construire* is valid for two years. It can be extended if you give notice two months before the initial two year deadline is reached. Work has to have been physically started and not just informed as having been started within the valid period.

NOTIFICATION OF WORK TO BE CARRIED OUT (*DÉCLARATION DE TRAVAUX*)

The official notification form must be lodged and a receipt obtained, or sent by registered post, to the town hall, indicating the work commencement date. This must be done at least one month before the commencement date.

As with the *permis de construire* an outside noticeboard must be displayed indicating that the town hall has received your notification and therefore authorised the work. The noticeboard must be displayed throughout the work period, and for at least two months, even if work is completed within two months. The non-display fine is €1,500.

The *déclaration de travaux* is valid for two years, and cannot be extended if work has not actually started within this period.

Taxation liabilities following construction work, particularly if it adds to the *surface habitable*, are detailed in Chapter 16.

Part Two

Renovating Your Property

This part of the book assumes that you have taken into account any estate regulations and the town planning density and general building regulations described in the previous chapters. Do not forget, that **before** starting any work you must comply with the procedures for planning permission or notification, if applicable.

6

Extensions and Verandas

We have seen in the previous chapter that the size of the projected floor area will determine whether a *permis de construire* or simple *déclaration de travaux* is required and also whether an architect is necessary.

Why do you want this additional floor area? Is it for a bright office, perhaps for professional reasons, or for a sober and quiet study? Do you want to make the most of the spring and summer months to have a better view of and easier access to the garden, or of the autumn and winter months just to have a pleasant view outside? Do you need an extra lounge, new dining room or more bedrooms?

Your answers will help you to decide if an extension or veranda (which is assumed to be an enclosed area like a conservatory) suits you better. Perhaps you need both. Heating requirements, wall and ceiling insulation and choice of window design, types and quality are all considerations. The position of the room(s) is also important, allowing for any structural limitations imposed by the topography of your land.

Both extensions and verandas are covered by the 10-year construction work guarantee (*garantie décennale*), provided that all the work is carried out by a professional builder, who must have appropriate insurance cover. If possible, use builders on an approved list (see Chapter 14). The 10-year guarantee covers any defects which threaten the solidity of the construction or correct functioning of its integral (*indissociable*) fixtures, e.g. a bath. Even if the problem is due to soil subsidence, see 'Foundations' below, you are covered.

The property owner benefiting from the work is the *maître d'ouvrage* and the builder or supervising architect is the *maître d'oeuvre*.

EXTENSIONS

You may well be a competent professional builder, but unless you have professional building insurance valid in France as a registered builder or are certain that you will not be reselling the property within 10 years of having completed the extension, you are advised to employ a professional who *is* in business. You'll be able, anyway, to keep an experienced eye on work in progress.

Foundations

Professional or not, you should beware of building an extension on any up-sloping side of your property. The new construction can block the natural down-flow of rainwater, which may dry out the existing foundations, encouraging wall cracks and worse. As a general rule, avoid cementing the new construction to the old. Allow for any play between the old and new walls by using a rubber-based joining agent which permits flexibility.

Ensure that the new foundations respect the anti-frost depth norms **plus** 20 to 30 cm. The anti-frost depth norms are the soil depths to which water can freeze. The foundations should therefore go down to the **norm-plus** depth to combat the 'softening' effect on soil when prolonged frost thaws out. The depths vary with the climate and soil. The norms (to which should be added the 20 to 30 cm) are:

Côte d'Azur, Corsica, parts of Britanny and of Normandy	0.25 m
Mediterranean, Atlantic and most of the Channel coasts	0.40 m
West France, the Pyrenees and part of Rhône-Alpes	0.50 m
Central France strip (from north to south) and the Southern Alps	0.60 m
Most of eastern France, excluding Lorraine and north Champagne	0.70 m
North Champagne, Lorraine and Upper Savoy	0.80 m
Alsace region and Nord *département*	0.90 m

Although the norm-plus depths are calculated for two floors, it is recommended that you use them for one level, i.e. ground floor, extensions. Check with your builder. Hilly areas are colder, so increase these depths by .05 m (5 cm) for every 200 m increase in altitude.

Walls

An aeration grill should be set into an outside wall between the floor level and the soil (the *vide sanitaire*).

Building blocks will be: brick (*brique*); breeze-blocks (*parpaings*) or air-entrained concrete (*béton cellulaire*) blocks subsequently finished with a stucco coating; or cut stone or open stone-work (*pierre apparente*) like flint walls; all depending on style and regional regulations. Breeze-blocks have two categories: load-bearing and non-load-bearing. Make sure load-bearing ones (*pour élévation de mur porteur*) are used. *Béton cellulaire* blocks have good insulating qualities, weigh less than breeze-blocks and are quicker to build with, but they do work out about twice as expensive.

Minimum insulation for outside walls is completed on the inside by a 0.06 m (6 cm) thick polystyrene sheet, or similar, plus a 1 cm thick plasterboard.

With open stone-work it is tricky to ensure a soundly constructed wall, unless you're investing in massive blocks of stone. It is usually now used only as a decorative facing on the outside or inside of load-bearing breeze-block or air-entrained concrete block walls, or for garden walls.

If your extension includes two rooms such as a lounge and a bedroom, sound insulation between them needs special consideration. Partition walls (*cloisons*) of 5 cm thick composed of two plaster boards (*plaques de plâtre*) sandwiching a 'honeycomb' bakelite centre (*résille en carton bakelisée*) provide excellent heat insulation but are notoriously low on sound-proofing. The ideal solution is a solid wall like the outside wall(s) completed by heat insulating materials (*construction traditionnelle*).

Windows

Size and type will depend largely on whether the room is a bedroom or daytime room and also on whether the façade faces the sun, the wind or the north.

Will you choose wood, PVC or aluminium frames? Wood is the cheapest, but requires maintenance. PVC is next in price and realistic wood simulations exist. This is an excellent idea, incidentally, for restorations (see Chapter 10) if you're prepared to sacrifice authenticity for easy maintenance. Aluminium is the top of the range, offering guarantees of up to 20 years, and rigid frameworks for large plate-glass sliding doors. If you're installing glass sliding doors, gain interior wall space by finishing the wall with a double skin so that the doors slide into it and not in front of it. All types include up to 24 mm double-glazing, sandwiching argon gas, which claims to reduce heating bills by around 10 per cent. See also 'Windows' in Chapters 7 and 8.

Ceilings and roofs

A flat roof, tiled or with a pebbledash coating (*crépi granité*), with a slight downward slope towards the ground, will be usual for an extension which is simply ground floor. For re-roofing a tiled sloping roof see Chapter 9. Consider putting up guttering – although some *cahier des charges* frown on it as being unsightly if it's facing the road and other houses – to stop the rain flowing off your existing sloping roof onto the extension's roof.

Ceiling insulation will be required even if the extension is not going to be used all year round. Rockwool (*laine de roche*) or glass fibre (*laine de verre*) are still the most cost-effective insulating materials. The latest products are recycled paper rockwool and 'user friendly' (they don't irritate the skin or lungs) duck feather eiderdown fibres. Consult the thermal coefficients which are given on the packaging and do your sums. Composite slabs of plasterboard backed by rockwool or glass fibre are a good solution. These will be fitted to the ceiling joists from the inside of the room, as loft height will be almost non-existent, using special screws (*vis*). This is something you could do yourself, provided you don't damage the structural work (and your 10-year guarantee).

Heating
Will you choose integration with the existing heating system, wall-fitted and thermostatically controlled appliances or mobile units to be used occasionally? Room aspects, climate, insulation, daytime or evening usage or both: all have a bearing on your decision.

Why not first 'test the temperature' during the cold months with an odourless mobile oil or paraffin stove (*poele à mazout* or *à pétrôle*) – cheap to buy, from around €100? Then decide what you need long term: an open or glass-fronted fireplace if a chimney is possible; a storage heater (*accumulateur de chaleur*) from around €500 and extremely effective if well positioned; a radiant heater (*radiateur rayonnant*) which costs less; or classic electric convectors from around €60 each. If you're in the Mediterranean area, inland south-west regions up to Bordeaux or in a continental (hot in summer, cold in winter) climate zone, which includes large towns like Strasbourg, some form of air-conditioning is desirable in the summer months.

Partition walls with plaster-board insulation slabs or solid walls similarly insulated are easy to drill holes in for passing pipes or installing plug points. You may qualify for a rebate on the cost, from the national electricity (*EDF*) or national gas (*GDF*) boards, especially if the work is undertaken at the same time as improvements to the property's existing heating system. Check with the local office. (From 1 July 2004, electricity supply to businesses will no longer be the monopoly of the *EDF* and from 1 July 2007, the domestic users' market will also be open to other electricity suppliers.)

VERANDAS

A veranda (or conservatory) can be beautiful to look at, but is it going to be an unbearable hothouse in summer and freezing cold in winter? Today, you can find veranda designs and materials that will give you thermal insulation and brightness, combining the feeling of being in the open air with the comfort of being inside your property – quicker and perhaps cheaper than an extension.

You're unlikely to need an architect or builder as any self-respecting veranda company will have its own show room (*salle d'exposition*) with walk-through examples of the main types shown in its catalogue, and a team of specialised installers (*poseurs specialisés*).

Verandas can be sub-divided into three main designs: the simple 'lean-to' (*en appui*); the semi-circular or multi-sided (*rayonnante*); and the Victorian conservatory cathedral style (*Victorienne*) complete with wrought iron roof trimmings. Companies that have their own factory will make your veranda to order following your measurements and specifications. 'Lean-tos' are the most economical and ideal if you already have a solid end wall, and a terrace or patio area. You can also easily run them parallel to two exterior walls to form an L shape. There will be little wastage on glass cuts as most of the panels will be rectangular. *Rayonnantes* cost more as there will be more glass wastage and their assembly will take longer. A long stretch of 'lean-to' with a protruding *rayonnante* section is attractive. *Victoriennes* are the most prestigious and, because of their complexity, size and differing glass cuts, the most costly.

Foundations

Unless you're building a half-walled (with thermal insulation as for an extension) and half-windowed veranda, an existing terrace or patio should support the weight of the glass, framework and any other insulating panels. But check with your supplier. They should visit you anyway, before accepting your order, to verify your measurements and approve the practicability of your plan, as their 10-year guarantee is on the line. Depending on the condition of the existing tiles you may want to re-lay the floor.

Your veranda may be a self-contained annexe to the property with access only from the garden, outside. It will still, in this case, be subject to the building regulations described in the previous chapter.

Choice of materials, heating and insulation

As for extensions, aluminium frames are best for the sliding windows which are an essential feature. If, and it is not recommended, you have bought the materials for the veranda independently of the installer, at least ensure that they have a 10-year guarantee. Clear glass should have 20 mm thick double glazing, particularly for the roof, unless you want greenhouse conditions whenever there's any prolonged sun. Double-glazing, with wood or simulated wood frames, for other windows comes into its own during the cooler months. A south-facing veranda with daytime usage in the spring and summer may need no interior heating. A radiator is a good solution otherwise.

Composite rectangular roof panels, 5 cm thick, exist. They are smooth and light in colour on the ceiling side, with a central slab of insulating material, reflecting heat from inside or outside. Exteriors are resistant to golf ball or giant hailstone impacts and they brighten the room, although they are opaque, so they exclude overwhelming sunlight. They can be tailored to *rayonnante* and *Victorienne* designs, so there is no reason why a Victorian veranda cannot integrate perfectly with a Provençal character house flooded with sunlight.

Verandas will leak if the join with the original property is not perfect and a defective join may not be obvious when you sign that the work has been finished to your complete satisfaction (the *garantie de parfait achèvement*). An obligatory clause in the guarantee gives you one year to discover any imperfections. A quick test is simple with a garden hose, preferably using a spray nozzle!

Useful vocabulary

accumulateur de chaleur	storage heater
brique	brick
cloison	partition wall
construction traditionnelle	solid walls with thermal insulation panels
crépi granité	pebbledash
double vitrage	double glazing
garantie décennale	10-year guarantee
garantie de parfait achèvement	work completed satisfactorily guarantee
gouttières	guttering
laine de roche	rockwool
laine de verre	glass fibre
mur porteur	load-bearing wall
panneau composite isolant	composite insulating panel
parpaing	breeze-block
pierre apparente	open stonework
plaques de plâtre	plasterboard
poele à mazout	oil stove
poele à pétrôle	paraffin heater
poseur	installation person
profondeurs de garde au gel	(anti-) frost depth norms
salle d'exposition	show-room
véranda en appui	'lean-to' veranda
véranda rayonnante	semi-circular or multi-sided veranda
vide sanitaire	space between earth and floor level
vis	screw

7

Conversions

Aménagement, as regards building work, has a wide meaning. It can mean:

◆ fitting out with equipment, so the room (which has already been converted) can better serve its purpose

◆ converting, in the traditional attic conversion sense

◆ with kitchens, for example, putting in the plumbing necessary for dishwashers and washing machines.

Reading property advertisements therefore needs attention. Don't miss out on something suitable because you thought there was too much conversion work to do. A property with *grand sous-sol aménageable* and *cuisine à aménager* should mean there is a large basement floor which can be converted and, strictly speaking, an old kitchen which would benefit from extra inlet and outlet pipes. You won't have to create a kitchen.

French '*lofts*' are converted spacious through-rooms, often with lofty ceilings and large skylights: top floors of old apartment blocks or disused factory floors in areas now fashionable. They are ideal for artists working from home or open-plan offices.

This chapter concerns conversion of existing floor space in the residential part of a property – the main house – to habitable or utility rooms: attic floors to bedrooms or studies, garages to extra rooms or self-contained apartments, basement areas to garages, games-rooms, wine cellars . . . (Outhouse conversions are described in Chapter 12.)

Floor areas of attics and basement areas which have been converted will not be liable for property taxation if their ceiling heights are below 1.80 m. They cannot officially produce additional habitable or business usage floor area (*surface habitable*). So if you have a registered business which operates from premises with a ceiling height of below 1.80 m you are flouting the law – even if you never receive any business visitors and only measure 1.60 m (5ft 3ins).

ATTICS

Professional architectural inspiration may be dispensed with, but if the room was previously a hay-loft, a classic low-roofed attic or a poky maid's bedroom (*chambre de bonne*) under the eaves of a fine townhouse (*maison bourgeoise*) the conversion possibilities will differ. You will of course have previously checked that the property's foundations are adequate (see Chapter 4, page 35).

Grenier (hay or grain-loft)

These are ideal for an extra lounge, TV room or holiday apartment with light furniture. The creation of an elevated sleeping area against a wall, like a wide wall shelf with beams to delimit the side and end of the bed, is a practical way of gaining floor space. Keep any original outside access, which will be extremely useful for moving in any furniture, or if you want a self-contained unit. Install a spiral staircase (*escalier en colimaçon*) to save space and stop the dog from going further upstairs, if it's an integral part of your main accommodation. Don't skimp on the width of the spiral staircase, otherwise large friends and family visitors may not be able to negotiate the staircase, unless that's what you want! The standard diameter of a spiral staircase is around 1.80 m.

Combles (attics)

These are ideal for a spacious children's bedroom as the ceiling apex may not permit an adult to stand up, or, with a partition wall, two small bedrooms for occasional visitors. Velux windows are simple to install in the sloping roof.

Chambre de bonne (garret)

These were among the first bedrooms with sloping ceilings (*chambres mansardées*) and small slightly protruding dormer windows (*chiens-assis*) or tiny sky-lights (*vasistas*), the walls and ceilings were bare of wood panelling (*lambris*), often used in renovations and conversions today. They are ideal for a study, away from the bustle and noise of the living rooms and kitchen. The windows may need modernising and, if they are *vasistas*, enlarging. There is standing room for an adult, but the rooms are not large enough for comfortable bedrooms, unless you knock down a dividing wall. Check it's not a load-bearing one.

Heating, insulation and soundproofing

Approximately 30 per cent of heat loss in properties is through attics, ceilings and roofs. Heat loss through walls, discounting window areas, is estimated at 15 per cent. Getting your choice of insulating materials right is important.

Before starting any work, check that the roof and timber framework is sound (see 'Re-roofing' in Chapter 9).

Then tackle the ceiling insulation. Leave an airspace of between 3 to 5 cm between the roof or its interior lining and the roof side of the insulating material. As with extension ceilings, composite slabs or panels of plaster board, backed by rockwool or glass fibre, are recommended. Fix the panels between – if you want to have 'open' rafters – or onto the rafters using special screws (*vis*) or a clipping system (*clipsage*). A face dust-mask is advisable if you have to cut or trim the panels using a small cutting knife (*cutter*) rather than a saw.

In attics, if what was previously the ceiling of the rooms below was insulated between the joists, it may be worth reclaiming and re-laying some of the material in the inaccessible areas where the roof comes down to the floor, i.e. beyond what is going to be the new, boarded floor area. Do this, of course, before putting up any insulating wall panels. Machine propulsion of rockwool granules into inaccessible corners is another solution.

Particular attention to the type and thickness of the insulating materials used is vital for wall insulation. Is there a north-facing wall which demands thicker insulation? If you're installing a kitchenette or bathroom the material must allow for aeration and be waterproof (*matériau hygrophobe*). Old walls in a period property or a hayloft are often irregular and manufacturers such as Knaufinsulation have an extensive range of products enabling flat false walls, or ceilings, to be created, using timber frames, insulating materials and internal 'dry' panelling over an irregular base. Visit the website at www.knaufinsulation.com for product descriptions in English and then consult 'France' and your *département*, e.g. 75 for Paris, for local distributors.

A most effective soundproofing material is a composite panel consisting of two outside plasterboards sandwiching a central strip of glass fibre or similar heat insulating material. This is a good choice if you're insulating a garret room study from outside noise. As an indication, a composite panel of two strips of plasterboard, each 7.5 cm thick, sandwiching a 4.5 cm thick glass fibre centre, is completely soundproof up to 48 decibels – modern washing machine noise level – assuming a 500 hertz (sound frequency) level. Double-glazing for windows is essential. A bedroom next to a living room or the next door neighbours in a semi-detached (*maison mitoyenne*) may still suffer from excessive noise despite using this material. Reinforce the soundproofing with slim, less than 5 cm thick, rigid plastic boards – Placosilence, for example – which are easily screwed into place after you have cut them to size.

These insulating and soundproofing principles hold good for garage, semi-basement and ground floor conversions, if required. Bear in mind that you should insulate the ceiling of a new or existing garage if you create a living room or bedroom above it.

GARAGE CONVERSIONS

Occasional use for purposes other than a garage, provided you have not changed or added windows or exterior doors, will not require any authorisation or notification.

If your car never leaks oil or you have adequate protective ground sheeting, there are no restrictions on tiling the floor (*réfection du sol*) so you have a dance floor – French people love dancing – for parties, particularly if drinks and food are in an adjacent kitchen. A simple step ladder or stairs to an elevated storage or work area is also feasible if you have a high-ceilinged or sloping roof garage with upper level windows.

Double garages, around 30 m², lend themselves to apartment or studio conversions. If this additional accommodation is for summer lets only or just for visiting friends and family the insulation work need not be elaborate, as auxiliary heating, such as convectors or radiators, can be plugged in. Existing windows may need to be replaced or new windows created and proper flooring laid over the existing concrete. The garage door, if you are letting, should be replaced by a front door or sliding plate glass windows.

The ceiling heights, if you let the apartment, of all main and utility rooms should be at least 2.30 m. For letting purposes the apartment must also have a *surface habitable* of at least 16 m² which rules out many single garages which are 15 m². The average surface area of the main rooms must be at least 9 m², with no main room under 7 m². This excludes the kitchen or kitchenette, and a linear 3 × 2 m (6 m²) kitchenette with single sink, fridge, washing machine, work surfaces and wall cupboards is a sensible size for studios or small apartments (see 'Kitchens' in Chapter 8). Letting accommodation must include a shower room or bathroom and a WC. Partition walls are the solution for separating the rooms.

Check if there are any regulations or special procedures concerning car ports (*abris de voiture*) if you want to put one up.

Perhaps you have a double garage and you could benefit from an extra room without having to extend the property. A long 'through' garage is ideal for a secluded room at the back, with French windows, leading to the garden and not onto the road or facing properties. Use non load-bearing breeze-blocks (*parpaings pour murs non porteurs*) in preference to partition panels as a solid crash barrier for the new interior wall, just in case you engage first gear instead of reverse, or vice-versa, when starting up the car. Complete, with appropriate wall panels for heating insulation and soundproofing, as for attics.

BASEMENTS

Perhaps you have bought a long Alpine barn set on a long slope providing a useful basement area, or a 30-year-old house anywhere with a basement (*sous-sol*) or semi-basement floor with basement windows (*fenêtres de sous-sol*). The conversion possibilities and methods will differ, but the first consideration is common to all. Are the walls damp? Are there any cracks in the walls?

Assuming there are no obvious cracks going right through the walls, check for signs of surface repair work which may hide a deeper problem. An old property with unequal walls should be verified by a chartered surveyor (*géomètre*) or architect.

Problems with damp

If there is dampness, where is it coming from? A simple DIY test is to fix runs of aluminium sheeting to the interior (room side) of walls concerned and inspect them after a few days.

If dampness is on the room side of the sheeting, the problem is condensation. Insert wall aeration grills (*ouvertures/grilles d'aération*). Special wall-drying cylinders (*assécheurs de murs*), which should be facing out from the outside walls and placed about every 50 cm in a line approximately 20 cm above the ground, should also be inserted in the walls. If the wall side of the sheeting is damp then it's a damp-proofing problem. Dry the wall(s) and obtain specialist advice as to whether a water-proof coating (*enduit imperméabilisant*) should be applied or whether injection of a special resin-based cement which absorbs water (*mortier de résine à diffusion lente*) would be a better solution, depending on the extent of the problem. Lead sheeting (*papier au plomb*) applied like wallpaper is another solution. Damp-proofing can create a drainage problem so ask how drainage could be improved. If both sides of the aluminium sheeting are damp you have both problems.

Injection of a fungicide product (*fungicide curatif*) in interior walls is necessary if fungi are present and in-growing. If fungi are only on the surface, burn them off with a blowlamp. The areas concerned should be well aired out beforehand. Fungi can also attack roof rafters. Dampness may also be due to gutter leaks, leaking roofs (see Chapter 9), badly fitting windows or drainage/canalisation leaks.

Repairs or replacements and drying out of surfaces in general is best done in spring so that surfaces can be damp-proofed in summer when they're really dry.

Different uses of basements
A **semi-basement** floor running under the whole property, with some basement windows and sloping access from outside, is well-suited to provide at least garaging for one car (5×3 m), a boiler room (if you're re-doing the heating system and want a bit more space in the house) and a games area – at least 6×2.5 m for table tennis, but much wider for full-size snooker – and/or a mini-gym. It is advisable to have the usual ceiling height of 2.30 m for the games/gym area for lifting weights or overhead smashes! Otherwise little alteration is required, apart from choosing a good garage door.

Double, folding, pull-up, sliding and 'up-and-over' doors – the choice is wide, in PVC, steel or wood. Very basic, non-insulated, 'up-and-over' single garage steel doors, in kit form, start at around €400. The same door, opening automatically, will cost about double. Top of the range door prices are around €2,000. Security and practicability (if your downward slope runs almost into the garage, a double or folding door won't be suitable) are key factors in choosing. Shock-absorbing rubber floor tiles (*dalles pour sols sportifs*), easily laid on concrete floors in games areas, are available from specialist manufacturers.

A **larger semi-basement** floor running under the entire property could be laid out as a single garage of 15 m² open to a small workshop area of 5 m² housing the boiler, and a further utility area, for games, also of 15 m², plus an occasional two-room granny flat of 25 m² *surface habitable*. Assuming, for example, that the property is a two-storey house with identical 60 m² floors this gives a total *surface habitable* of 145 m², the equivalent of a four-bedroom property with generous rooms. There are numerous permutations.

> Remember that employing an architect is obligatory above a total *surface habitable*, including the proposed conversion area, of 170 m².

An **entirely underground** floor, with access from inside or outside the house, is ideal for a wine cellar or reserve pantry. For a wine cellar the room should be dark and dry, with the temperature maintained around 14°C. Provide occasional lighting. There is no need to concrete the floor. Just level out the area and lay down a few solid paving stones so that you can install horizontal bottle racking or shelves for household provisions. Vaulted stone cellars in character properties are tailor-made wine cellars and probably were designed as such. A swimming pool (see Chapter 12) adjacent to the house can conveniently conceal its water filtration pump there. Access from outside and soundproofing are preferable.

GROUND-LEVEL FORMER STABLING, CATTLE SHEDS, WORK FLOORS OR SIMILAR

Where these can be the entrance floor to the residential part of the property they offer a multitude of conversion possibilities which can integrate perfectly with the existing accommodation. As the new entrance will open onto living area seen immediately by all visitors, using a local architect to create a living area in keeping with the property's style is recommended – especially where high ceilings suggest possibilities for semi-mezzanine areas and split-level floors. Installation of windows and doors will be necessary. If the wall facing the predominant wind is windowless, why not keep it so for better wind protection?

A large open-plan living floor (kitchen, dining room and lounge) is attractive. The open-plan can be broken up by partition walls with large arches, opening, for example, from the kitchen to the dining room, to the lounge. Heat insulation or soundproofing of these partitions is not essential and air-entrained concrete block tiles (*carreaux de béton cellulaire*) or water-repellent – for kitchens – plasterboard square tiles (*carreaux de plâtre hydrofuges*) are light and, being larger than breeze-blocks, quick to lay. Both *carreaux* types come in 'squares' of around 50 × 60 cm, usually 5 cm thick, and each have special cements (*colle-ciment*). DIY or not, work out your wall areas and compare non load-bearing breeze-blocks and *carreaux* prices before deciding which to use. Breeze-blocks need stucco coating to finish whereas *carreaux* can just be painted.

Safety and comfort will be key factors in the choice of stairs connecting this new living area floor to the upper floor. If the original outside steps to the old entrance are still in use, a spiral staircase (left- or right-turning) is *the* space-saver, but not best for comfort. Quarter turn staircases, turning at the bottom, middle or top, with or without a halfway landing area, are the next best space-savers. Ideally, a straight flight of stairs with comfortable long steps and an easy ascent angle requires a ceiling opening of around 4.50 m. However, if the available space you have is less than this, house *aménagement* companies, such as Lapeyre (www.lapeyre.fr) offer a made-to-measure service. If the stairs are going to be narrow and you have to move furniture upstairs from the inside of the property ask if removable banisters (*rampe d'escalier amovible*), which you can slot into and out of place when required, can be provided.

FLOOR COVERINGS

Choice of floor coverings, all applied directly or indirectly onto a concrete base – attics apart – depend on usage and insulation required. Make sure, whether you're preparing the floor or employing a contractor, that the concrete base is dry, clean and level. Use a cement type mix for levelling (*produit de ragréage*). In general, chipboard floor panels (*panneaux de particule pour sol*) are better for laying over old tiling or directly onto concrete. Hardboard floor panels (*panneaux de fibres pour sols*) are better suited for laying over old parquet. Chipboards are fixed with special screws and hardboards are glued.

Floor tiles are almost *de rigueur* for ground floor rooms south of Lyon, but the choice is yours. Because of their water resistant qualities they are the natural choice for kitchens, kitchenettes, shower rooms and bathrooms, and sensible – because they're easy to clean – for all ground level rooms or semi-basements with direct access from outside. The decorative aspect of tiling which gives authenticity to old buildings should not be overlooked. Floors, more than walls, tend to show up irregularities in laying and joining tiles, unless that's the effect you're seeking, so think twice before tackling the job yourself.

Main floor tile types

Enamelled sandstone tiles (**grés émaillés**)
Used principally for bathrooms, kitchens and living rooms. Hard-wearing, shock-resistant and impervious. Should not be waxed.

Terra cotta (**terre cuite**)
Interior use only. Hard-wearing, but less resistant to shocks than sandstone. Can be waxed. Should be coated with an anti-porosity agent after being laid down.

Stone (**pierre**)
Hard-wearing and shock-resistant. Easy to clean with detergents.

Marble (**marbre**)
Extremely hard-wearing. Interior or exterior usage.

Vinyl rolls
Cheaper (and less attractive) than tiles. Ideal for rooms used occasionally.

Solid or imitation parquet flooring
In chestnut, oak, pine and hard exotic woods or finishes, now comes in all shapes, designs and sizes.

Laying flooring

Before laying any parquet or chipboard floor boards in attic areas being converted for the first time, measure the space between the joists. 60 cm is a **maximum** distance between joists. If they are wider apart get a roofing carpenter (*charpentier de toiture*) to add some joists or supporting beams. A full-scale attic room conversion with permanent furniture requires a qualified professional to lay the floor, not least to ensure that it is well nailed and not glued into position. (Laying a few loosely fitting boards for storing odd items is another matter.)

However, ground or basement floors can be laid with parquet or imitation parquet flooring by DIY enthusiasts. To ensure comfort and noiselessness underfoot a felt type underlay should be put down first of all. The parquet, supplied in tongued and grooved strips or squares, can then be fitted together without necessarily being glued together. Fitting and laying instructions, on the parquet packaging, are often in French and English.

Useful vocabulary	
abri de voiture	car port
assécheur de murs	wall-drying cylinder
buanderie	laundry room
carreau de béton cellulaire	air-entrained concrete block tile
carreau de plâtre hydrofuges	water-repellent plasterboard tile
cave au vin	wine cellar
chambre de bonne	garret
chambre mansardée	bedroom with sloping roof
charpentier de toiture	roofing carpenter
chiens-assis	dormer windows
colle-ciment	cement glue

combles	attic
cuisine à aménager	kitchen requiring plumbing for appliances
cuisine aménagée	kitchen with plumbing for appliances
cuisine équipée	fitted kitchen
cutter	small knife with thin sharp blade
dalle en caoutchouc pour sols sportifs	shock-absorbing rubber tile for sports floors
enduit imperméabilisant	waterproof coating
escalier en colimaçon	spiral staircase
fenêtre de sous-sol	basement half-window
fungicide curatif	fungicide for wall injection
grenier	(hay/grain) loft
gré émaillé	enamelled sandstone tile
grille d'aération	wall aeration grill
lambris	wood panelling
loft	large studio apartment, usually top floor
maison bourgeoise	fine townhouse
maison mitoyenne	semi-detached house
masque	mask
matériau hygrophobe	waterproof material
mortier de résine à diffusion lente	slow-spread, water absorbant resin-based cement
panneau de particules, pour sols	chipboard floor panel
panneau de fibres, pour sols	hardboard floor panel
papier au plomb	lead sheeting
parpaing pour murs non porteurs	non-load-bearing breeze-block
pierre	stone
produit de ragréage	liquid cement-type mix for floor levelling
réfection du sol	repairing/renovating/re-laying the floor
sous-sol	basement
terre cuite	terra cotta

8

Complete Transformation and Redesign

If complete transformation and redesign are your aims, your property will probably fall into one of three broad categories:

1. A completely gutted building with, or without, existing floors.

2. A quite habitable building, perhaps an old village house or a large country house.

3. A large property previously used as a main home which you now wish to adapt to furnished apartments for long or short-term lets.

USING AN ARCHITECT

For each category you are advised to consult a local architect for any of the following purposes:

◆ To check what is a load-bearing wall and what is just a cleverly disguised partition wall, if you're putting in new floor levels, knocking down interior walls to create larger rooms or putting up interior walls to create bedrooms. (Village houses tend to have small rooms and old country houses sometimes have inter-connecting rooms.)

◆ To use their local knowledge and expertise for design and choice of materials. Something unusual may suit you, but if it's too off-beat it can reduce the market value of the property: an exaggerated example would be an arabesque bathroom, with a ceiling height of just 1.80 m, in a Provençal farmhouse. Consider for example the implications of doing without an existing second bathroom in a five bedroom house so that you can put in a sixth bedroom. Is it a wise decision? At least partition off and keep the plumbing for the bath, and put in a separate or *en suite* shower room.

◆ To co-ordinate the project and deal with builders. Competent general building companies offering brick-laying and plastering, carpentry, electrical, heating and tiling services are difficult to find, although, if you bought through an estate agent they may be able to recommend companies. Otherwise, you will no doubt have recourse to specialist individual companies. An architect will draw you a blueprint, and, as *maître d'oeuvre*, advise you on estimates, co-ordinate the work and approve it as it proceeds, giving you the go-ahead to pay contractors' invoices if it has been agreed to pay in stages, and get the best result overall in terms of design and use of the available space. Ask to see similar projects the architect has master-minded. Their services cost around 12 per cent of your building costs. Your building costs could be 12 per cent more if you don't employ one.

DEMOLITION PERMITS

Planning to partly demolish and re-build on the same spot? A demolition permit (*permis de démolir*) is required in the Paris area (up to 50 km from the centre) and of course in conservation areas. Always check the situation at your local town hall, wherever you are, and at the same time see if the local planning coefficient (COS) or estate regulations, which may have changed since the original construction work, allow you to replace the previous *surface habitable*.

WORK COMPLETED REPORT DOCUMENTS

You should ask your architect to be present when you, as the *maître d'ouvrage* (owner and beneficiary of the construction work) sign off the work as being completed: the *procès-verbal de réception* (work completed report document). The *garantie de parfait achèvement* (satisfactorily completed work guarantee) runs from that time and gives you one year to discover any imperfections that were not apparent when you signed off the work. This guarantee is completed of course by the 10-year guarantee – see the beginning of Chapter 6 – and the *garantie biennale/de bon fonctionnement* (two-year guarantee) which covers all items and equipment, such as taps, boilers, blinds, doors and electrical equipment, which can be removed without damaging the building structurally.

There is no standard wording for the *procès-verbal de reception*, but it must be signed and dated by you and the contractor, with your names and addresses, stipulating the work completed and the address of the property concerned. Key phrases should include:

Après avoir visité les lieux et examiné les travaux réalisés par (the name of the company) *le maître d'ouvrage* (you) *en présence du représentant de* (the company) *déclare accepter les travaux.*

(In summary: you have inspected the work done by the company in the presence of their representative and accept it.)

Il reconnait que celui-ci est conforme au contrat conclu.

(In summary: you agree that the work corresponds to your agreement with the contractor.)

A compter de ce jour commence également à courir les délais de garanties que (the company) *s'engage à assurer:*
  – *Garantie de parfait achèvement*
  – *Garantie de bon fonctionnement*
  – *Garantie/responsabilité décennale* (if applicable)

(In summary: the statutory guarantees are effective from today.)

Sous reserve de . . . (List any appliances or materials you have not been able to check. This list will not affect your rights if any defects become apparent later on in the guarantee periods.)

A *procès-verbal* should be signed for each individual contractor.

The work planned will almost certainly involve bedroom fittings, wardrobes and new storage space, creating or re-designing kitchens, bathrooms and shower rooms, and choice and installation of new windows.

Useful vocabulary

garantie biennale/de bon fonctionnement	two-year guarantee
garantie de parfait achèvement	satisfactorily completed work guarantee
permis de démolir	demolition permit
procès-verbal de réception	work completed report document

BEDROOMS

If the property you are buying does have a fitted (permanently fixed) bedroom, and not just built-in cupboards, stipulate in the *promesse de vente* and *acte authentique* that this remains fixed if you want it. Fitted bedrooms, a huge market in the UK, are rare in France and when found are likely to be of excellent quality, and therefore costly to replace, having been custom-built by an *ébéniste* (a skilled cabinet-maker). Property sales in France do not usually include 'fixtures' (permanently fixed items) **and** 'fittings' (removable items). What you thought was a 'fixture', for example a fitted bedroom, may be transformed into a 'fitting' before you take possession, if you're not careful.

Modular, free-standing wardrobes and cupboards are the French rule, with adjustable hanging rails and interchangeable units. The great advantages are flexibility and the possibility of additional units as your requirements develop or change. Certain companies such as Sogal, Archea and Quadro (see Useful Websites for information and shop addresses) do, however, specialise in made-to-measure modern wardrobe units which will adapt to your floor and wall space. Large furniture stores, such as Habitat and Ikea, have attractive self-assembly units of good quality in light solid pine woods that you can buy off-the-shelf. The Conforama furniture shops, at the lower end of the market, are unbeatable on price. Stores like Monsieur Meuble have classic designs in hard exotic woods and French favourites, *chêne* (oak), *merisier* (cherry wood) and *noyer* (walnut).

A good size for a master bedroom is 15 m² if you're planning an extensive range of wardrobes or cupboards. A self-contained or partitioned off wardrobe room (*dressing*) occupying 4–5 m² is no doubt the French answer to the requirement for a fitted unit. A local *ébéniste* will certainly provide an elegant individual solution. Obtain three estimates (*devis*) for a sensible comparison of price and quality. Another idea is two bedrooms, linked by a *dressing*: a wardrobe for both rooms. Between 25 and 30 m² overall is the space required. If other bedrooms are *mansardées* (with sloping roofs down to the floor) use the 'lost' floor space for low-level drawers and cupboards.

A mezzanine sleeping area for children, over wardrobes, or in a study over a desk, is a practical solution for gaining extra space and perhaps an extra bedroom. Particularly high ceilings in a spacious room suggest mezzanine floor possibilities. Consult your architect.

Planning your bedroom layout in relation to the living rooms is an obvious part of your architect's brief if total room layout is required. You may not have lived in a one-level bungalow (*maison à plain-pied*) before. Ideally, the bedrooms occupied all year round should be as far away as possible from the lounge and dining room. Fit a solid door, with good sound insulation, in the hall or corridor separating kitchen and living areas from bathroom and bedrooms. If bedrooms are upstairs, locating the master bedroom over the kitchen – breakfasts are quiet meals – rather than over the lounge is a good choice.

Useful vocabulary	
chêne	oak
devis	estimate
dressing	wardrobe room
ébéniste	cabinet maker
maison à plein pied	one-level house (bungalow)
merisier	wild cherry wood
noyer	walnut

KITCHENS

Assuming that the property does not have a large farmhouse kitchen (over 15 m²), the four kitchen layout plans on page 79 will guide you in your design and fitting out (*aménagement*).

The L-shaped, U-shaped and double linear kitchen layouts are each based on the 'triangular' principle of walking as little as possible between cooking, washing and storage areas. Space allows for intervening worktops, and foldaway breakfast bars are set against bare walls if there is no room for a centrally positioned table. If you plan to have patio windows, allow space for opening the refrigerator door. Make sure also that there is sufficient space to stand in front of refrigerators (approx. 80 cm), dish washers (approx. 90 cm) and ovens or floor standing cookers (at least 1 m) to be able to use them safely and comfortably. Under-floor plumbing may be necessary if the sink and dishwasher are on facing walls.

Draw up a to-scale plan before you contact fitted kitchen companies so that you can judge if their suggestions for your kitchen are sensible. A good professional should propose the following unit measurements and wall-fitted heights:

◆ **Wall cupboards.** Bottom of the door between 1.30–1.50 m above the floor. Depth, 32–40 cm.

L Shape
(7.60 m² in this example)
Two walls with appliances, cupboards and worktops.
Fold-down wall bar for breakfast.

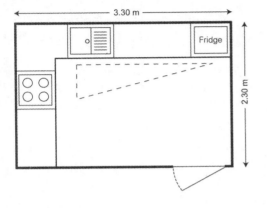

Double 'linear'
(9.80 m² in this example)
Long and sufficiently wide for table, seating
three, in the middle. Cooker/sink opposite
fridge and dishwasher.

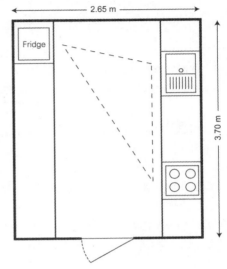

U Shape
(10.90 m² in this example)
Three walls with appliances, cupboards and
worktops. Breakfast table, for 4–6 people, in the
middle. At least 10 m² needed.

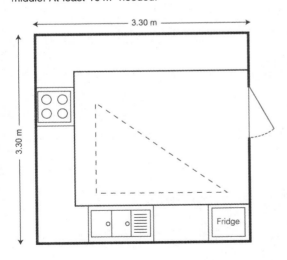

Single 'linear'
(7.40 m² in this example)
Long and narrow. Over 3 m long and 2 m
wide, max. Fold-down breakfast wall bar.
No work area triangle.

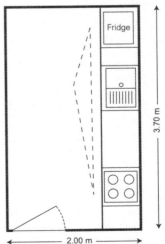

Figure 8   Kitchens.

- **Oven.** If you have children, don't have this floor-standing, but rather, wall-integrated, between a floor and wall unit. Have a glass door so you can see how things are cooking!

- **Floor units with worktops.** The standard height is 90 cm. Choose adjustable legs so you can vary the height to suit you. Depth: normally 65 cm.

- **Wall breakfast bar** width should be at least 40 cm. For a table with diners facing each other, allow for at least 70 cm.

French, Italian, British and German manufactured kitchens can be viewed in kitchen outlets – *cuisinistes*. Consult the display advertisements in the *Pages Jaunes*: *cuisines – ventes, installations*. Note that *cuisinistes* often have an exclusive franchise for their area for a manufacturer, especially for foreign manufacturers, so comparing estimates for identical fitted kitchens is difficult. An example of an estimate (*devis*) which is normally free, showing the information it should contain, is given further below. Prices are not indicated as these depend on the quality of the material.

There is an enormous choice on the market, from top of the range Bulthaup designer kitchens to self-assembly kitchen unit packs. Obtain three estimates for similar quality kitchens for the same amount of units to see if their estimates contain this basic information and also for an evaluation of a reasonable price for a satisfactorily completed job. Beware of fantastic discount companies. Will the quality of the installation be satisfactory? Look for at least a five-year guarantee of the material for the kitchen units fitted. Check whether worktops are heat-proof. Do you want tiled worktops? Think about rounding the splash area angles between walls and worktops and sink tops so that liquid spills and splashes and also crumbs can be easily wiped up.

Estimate for a fitted kitchen (*devis*)

Cuisiniste name and address, etc.   Town and date

Company registration number (N° *siret*)   Your name and address

Devis gratuit (free estimate)

Delivery and installation address (Your address)

Meubles (kitchen units and catalogue model)

> *Porte* (door) with description of composition of the material, thickness, finish and colour
> *Caisson* (kitchen wall or floor unit) with colour
> *Poignée* (handle) with catalogue description
> *Tiroirs* (drawers) if applicable, with catalogue description

1. Then the catalogue **reference number**, followed by a **description** of the unit, with left or right-opening doors, number of shelves, etc. and unit dimensions (e.g. height/*hauteur* 90 cm, width/*largeur* 60 cm, depth/*profondeur* 65 cm). (Wall unit: *élément haut*, floor unit: *élément bas*, sink cupboard unit: *bas sous-évier*)

Quantité (number of units) × price per unit . . . . Total TTC: xxx€

2. **Idem** for any other units or worktops (*plan de travail*) . . . . Total TTC: xxx€

Appareils ménagers (kitchen appliances)
Reference number
Lave-vaisselle (dishwasher) with **description** of programmes and decibels rating
Quantité . . . . Total TTC: xxx€

Reference number
Lave-linge (washing machine) with laundry weight **capacity**
Quantité . . . . Total TTC: xxx€

Evier (sink)
Reference number
Description, single or double, stainless steel, mixer taps, etc.
Quantité . . . . Total TTC: xxx€

Travaux (plumbing and electricity work)
> *Raccordements plomberie* (connection to **existing** plumbing, i.e. no new pipes)
> Total TTC: xxx€

> *Raccordements éléctriques* (electrical connection, with no new electrical work)
> Total TTC: xxx€

Livraison (delivery charge)
> *Total livraison* . . . . TTC: xxx€

Pose (fitting)

Installation of kitchen units. (Ensure that the *mise en service des appareils* – putting into service or testing of any kitchen appliances – is specified here).

Total pose et mise en service . . . . TTC: xxx€

Sommaire (summary)

Meubles . . . . TTC: xxx€

Appareils ménagers . . . . TTC: xxx€

Sanitaires (sinks, etc.) . . . . TTC: xxx€

Fournitures et accessoires (small sundries) . . . . TTC: xxx€

Travaux . . . . TTC: xxx€

Livraison . . . . TTC: xxx€

Pose et mise en service . . . . TTC: xxx€

Total devis   TTC: xxx€

Dont (of which) *TVA* (19.6%)   xxx€

Dont TVA (5.5%)   xxx€

If the delivery date and work completion date is not mentioned on the estimate make sure that they are stipulated on an order form (*bon de commande*) that is signed by you and the company.

Regulations and usual procedures regarding estimates in general are described in Chapter 16, as are the TVA ratings on property improvements and restoration. It is worth noting immediately, however, that kitchen **appliances** are always subject to 19.6 per cent TVA. On the other hand, if your property is more than two years old, and this applies to first or second homes, both the cost of kitchen **units** and their fitting charges when the work is done by a professional company or person who **also** supplied the units, are subject to the reduced rate of 5.5 per cent TVA, at least until the end of 2005. Free-standing mobile units, i.e. not fitted, do not qualify for 5.5 per cent TVA. They are TVA rated at 19.6 per cent. If the fitting charge is 'free' (but no doubt 'included' in the prices somewhere on the invoice) note that the TVA will be 19.6 per cent. A second grade kitchen invoiced in this way may cost nearly the same as a better quality kitchen for which you have been invoiced for the installation. Beware once again of special offers! You will also pay TVA at 19.6 per cent if you order a fitted kitchen and fit it yourself or have it fitted by a company other than the supplier.

Self-assembly kits for floor and wall units are available for the keen DIY person from *bricolage* (DIY) hypermarkets such as Castorama and LeRoy Merlin. The Ikea furniture stores and property *aménagement* companies like LaPeyre offer advice on fitting your *prêt à monter* (ready to assemble) kitchen units, as well as having their own *services de pose* (installation services) for fitted kitchens. Quality material can be found. All units are, of course, subject to TVA at 19.6 per cent if you install them yourself, but if you are confident, and competent, you can reduce the cost of your new kitchen considerably.

Useful vocabulary

appareils ménagers	kitchen appliances
bon de commande	order form
bricolage	DIY
caisson	open cupboard/cabinet, i.e. without doors
cuisinière	cooker
élément bas	floor unit
élément haut	wall unit
évier	sink
four (auto-nettoyant)	oven (self-cleaning)
hotte	extractor fan
lave-linge	washing machine
lave-vaisselle	dishwasher
meuble	furniture unit
plaque de cuisson	hob/cooking rings
poignée	handle
pose	fitting
prêt à monter	self-assembly kit
raccordement plomberie/ éléctricité	plumbing/electrical connection
tiroir	drawer

BATHROOMS

As with kitchens, unless you have lots of space, the design and layout of your bathroom(s) and shower room(s), interconnecting bathroom(s) or bathroom(s) with shower requires careful thought.

The six possibilities illustrated on page 85 are all designed for limited spaces, ranging from a mini-shower room, around 2 m², to a square bathroom, of around 5 m², with a large bath set into one corner and a WC or separate shower. All have wash basins or smaller hand basins and have a cupboard or storage unit. Room doors should open outwards, except for the largest (square) room. All washing machines must be earthed and placed at least 60 cm away from the outside edge of the bath or shower cubicle, which means a larger bathroom is necessary, or, ideally, a laundry room (*buanderie*) if the kitchen is not suitable. (See 'Reviewing the electrical installation' in Chapter 9 for details of electrical installation regulations for bathrooms.)

These are just suggestions. If two people need to wash at the same time, two wash basins or a double basin are possible if you don't need an extra cupboard or separate shower. And what about a bidet, which is extremely practical if you don't want to shower every time you wash your feet? Square shower cubicles are between 80–90 cm wide, single wash basins range from 55–90 cm wide and double wash basins are at least 1 m wide. Pre-set temperatures and adjustable nozzle spray pressures for showers provide comfort and economies and prevent scalding, and some wash and hand-basin taps (*robinetterie sanitaire*) now have slightly resistant levers that stop water gushing out when they're opened.

Hammam baths (traditional Arab baths, which are a combination of sauna and steam baths) can also be installed as they are available in cubicle form, like showers, starting from around 90 cm wide. If your proposed bathroom is a rectangular or square room of at least 5 m², why not install a bath with integrated shower tap, and a separate hammam? As hammams and sauna cabins are considered to be heating improvements, you may also qualify for tax relief – up to 31 December 2005 – off-set against their purchase prices (assuming, of course, that you pay income tax in France). The property must be your main residence and qualification depends on your family

Mini-shower room
Shower cubicle facing wash basin.

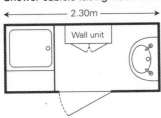

Square
Corner bath and wash basin. WC or shower cubicle.

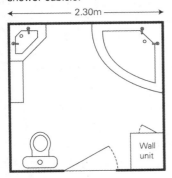

Linear
Assymetrical bath: easy access. Cupboard/basin unit.

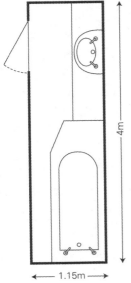

Interconnecting
Two adjacent bedrooms share shower cubicle. Hand basins in both bedrooms.

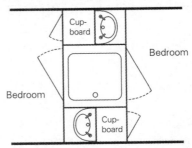

L Shape
Shower cubicle, WC and wash basin; all sensibly situated.

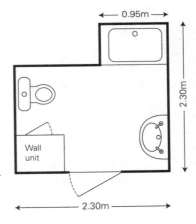

Rectangular
Standard bath and corner shower cubicle.

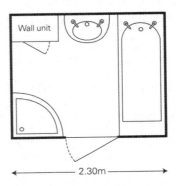

Figure 9   Bathrooms.

situation and your tax demand (*avis d'imposition*). You must also use the same company for the purchase and installation of the baths, so DIY enthusiasts are non-starters for this allowance.

Whatever type of bathroom you have in mind – Victorian retro, rustic or modern fitted – thoroughly check the walls (see 'Basements' in Chapter 7) for dampness, especially if you are creating a bathroom in an old property. The ventilation grill in an old property may be insufficient (or even non-existent) to cater for bathroom humidity. An automatic or manually controlled ventilation system (*ventilation mécanique contrôlée* or *VMC*) should be installed.

With the exception of the LaPeyre national chain (www.lapeyre.fr) and tile showrooms, fitted bathroom specialists dealing with the public can be difficult to find. If you have an architect for your overall project get them to accompany you to trade outlets and negotiate prices for you which will offset the higher rate of VAT, 19.6 per cent, you will have to pay if you, and not the tiler/plumber/fitter, are ordering the items. If, however, the professional carrying out the work is also the supplier, the items, with the exception of shelving which can be left free-standing, will be VAT rated at 5.5 per cent up to the end of 2005. Your property must be over two years old. The architect will also negotiate labour prices with the tiler, plumber and fitter. They will advise you on technical aspects such as the composition of material which will withstand cleansing solvents. If you're creating a bathroom in an old attic room bear in mind that a beautiful cast-iron pedestal bath weighing around 100 kgs (230 lbs) will severely test old floor joists. An acrylic bath, on the other hand, weighs around 20 kgs (50 lbs). More about floorings for bathrooms (and kitchens) below.

An example of how a free estimate for a fitted bathroom should be laid out follows. (This could be an estimate from LaPeyre. Or your architect has obtained estimates from a fitter and tiler, and a plumber, which together should contain this information.)

Estimate for a fitted bathroom (*devis*)

Company name and address   Town and date

Company registration number (*N° siret*)   Your name and address

Devis gratuit (free estimate) NB. LaPeyre charge €50 if they visit your home, which is deductible from their invoice if you give them the job.

Delivery and installation address

FOURNITURES (material)

Meubles (bathroom cabinets and catalogue model)

Ensemble. Bathroom range XXXXXX with bath (*baignoir*), taps to the left or right, washbasin with cabinet (*meuble sous vasque*), *portes* (catalogue style), colour. Dimensions of cabinets and wall units, with or without mirror, lighting, switch, etc.

> **Quantité** . . . . (Unit price exclusive of TVA) *Prix unitaire HT:* xxx€
>
> *Total* . . . . (Unit price × quantity, incl. of TVA) *TTC:* xxx€

Robinetterie (taps)

Description of types of taps (mixer, etc.) and material (chrome, etc.)

> **Quantité** . . . . (Unit price exclusive of TVA) *Prix unitaire HT:* xxx€
>
> *Total* . . . . (Unit price × quantity, incl. of TVA) TTC: xxx€

Carrelage (murs et sols): (tiles, or other coverings, for walls and floors)

Tile name. Dimensions, e.g. for tiles, 20 × 20 cm. Number of 25 tile packs, for example, and the total surface area they cover. (Due allowance should be made for wastage and joint widths according to complexity and design for the areas concerned.)

> *Prix unitaire* (per pack) HT: xxx€
>
> *Total* . . . . TTC: xxx€

Fournitures pour carrelage (tiling cement)
Brief description of cement, colour, bag weights and recommended surface coverage. Quantity ordered.

> *Prix unitaire* (per bag) HT: xxx€
>
> *Total* . . . . TTC: xxx€

Fournitures plomberie (plumbing material)
Brief description of length, diameter, type of metal, etc. of pipes. Quantity ordered.

Prix unitaire (each item) HT: xxx€

Total . . . . TTC: xxx €

Total fournitures (Total for material) . . . . TTC: xxx€

TRAVAUX (labour)

This may include:
Canalisations (canalisation work): modifying water outlets and fitting any new evacuation pipes or tubes;
Carrelage (tile laying and fixing);
Sanitaire (plumbing in and fitting): the bath(s), washbasin(s), and taps;
Meubles (fitting cabinets, mirrors, lights, etc.),
Travaux complementaires (other work specifically required).

Total travaux . . . . HT: xxx€
Total travaux . . . . TVA: xxx€
Total travaux . . . . TTC: xxx€

Total devis (fournitures et installation)   TTC: xxx€

If the delivery and work completion dates are not mentioned on the estimate, make sure that they are stipulated on an order form signed by you and the company.

Useful vocabulary

avis d'imposition	annual tax demand
baignoir	bath
buanderie	laundry room
douche	shower
équipement sanitaire	baths, wash basins, shower nozzles, taps, etc.
lavabo	wash basin
meuble sous vasque	integral wash basin cupboard unit
robinetterie	taps

BATHROOM AND KITCHEN FLOOR AND WALL COVERINGS

Hard-wearing, shock-resistant and impervious enamelled sandstone tiles (*grés émaillés*) remain the favourite choice for both kitchen and bathroom floors. They require little maintenance and are easily mop cleaned. Choose light, large tiles if you want to make the room appear bigger. Simulated wood laminates are another possibility for kitchens, as are PVC tiles. PVC is extremely hard-wearing, easy to lay and not expensive.

Marble is a de-luxe choice for bathroom floors. It is hard-wearing, but tends to stain, so is not a sensible choice for luxury kitchens. Exotic teak wood, as used on boat decks, is an attractive alternative to tiling bathroom floors. It does not deteriorate or fade and has natural anti-slip qualities. It should be laid by a teak specialist to ensure watertight joints. Look for labels indicating that it has not come from endangered forests. Vinyl and bathroom floor carpeting are cheaper alternatives. Floor tiles are heavy so take this into account if you are putting in a bathroom upstairs in an old property which has never had upstairs floor tiling.

Wall-tiling can be a DIY job when renovating a bare wall, but it is advisable to leave this to the fitter, or other professional, when they install a new kitchen or bathroom as they will best be able to co-ordinate tiling and wall unit and cabinet fitments so that the result doesn't look patchy. A new partition wall over any new plumbing going round the walls will save having to drill into existing brick walls. Large or small earthenware (*faience*) and enamelled terra cotta (*terre cuite émaillée*) wall tiles, depending on the effect desired, are ideal for both bathrooms and kitchens. Kitchens, in particular, can benefit from a wide range of floral or patterned designs to fit in with the property's general décor.

DOORS

Replacing doors is one of the simplest DIY jobs. Just a steady hand for dropping the new door onto the hinges and some assistance, if it's heavy, are required. Verify that the hinges are still in good order and the exact dimensions of the door. Your house contents insurance policy may stipulate that entrance and other outside house doors must be reinforced (*blindée*), fire-proof (*portes coupe feu*) and with at least three locking points when locked. Production line doors in wood, PVC or steel all have these specifications.

Don't forget to make the most of door designs which are typical of your area and to respect any limitations on style that may be imposed for outside doors. Apart from soundproofing between rooms, the heat insulating factor should not be neglected. Do you want solid wood doors or doors with glass panels for the living rooms, swing doors for the kitchen, or sliding doors for a dining or sleeping area?

For new door frames engage a carpenter (*menuisier*).

WINDOWS

The relative merits of wood, PVC or aluminium windows are described under the 'Extensions' section in Chapter 6.

But how do you want your different windows to open? A lot of houses have functional outside shutters and many insurance policies stipulate that shutters must be closed during the night if you want your insurance policy to cover theft. This probably explains why casement windows open inwards in France, enabling you to close shutters and keep windows open – a boon when there's a heat-wave. Iron grills over small windows of bathrooms, WCs, storerooms, etc. can replace shutters for insurance purposes. Horizontal and vertical pivoting, louvered, sash, sliding, and sliding folding windows are installed for bathrooms, kitchens, laundry rooms and other utility rooms as they are in the UK.

Installation of windows is best done by a registered contractor. This way the material and the installation is covered by the 10-year guarantee. (A leaking window is officially unacceptable in a habitation.) There is a multitude of local and national window companies. Among national companies which have their own factories and nationwide showrooms are HuisClos (www.huisclos.fr) and KparK (www.kpark.fr).

Do you want to brighten the room or lessen the brightness? Do you need translucent or clear windows? Sound and heat insulation are not the only considerations. If you are replacing single glazed windows by double glazing, will the existing aeration grills be sufficient?

Useful vocabulary	
fenêtre à guillotine	sash window
fenêtre à jalousies	louvered window
fenêtre à la française	casement window (opening inwards)
fenêtre basculante	horizontal pivoting window
fenêtre coulissante	sliding window
fenêtre en accordéon	sliding folding window
fenêtre en verre translucide granité	grained-look opaque window
fenêtre pivotante	vertical pivoting window

9

Renovation

This chapter covers the work that can be involved in properties advertised as *à rénover*. Renovation work might consinst of:

◆ Roofing renovation (or restoration).

◆ Elimination of asbestos materials (*désamiantage*) and lead-content paints (see 'Points to check' in Chapter 4). You may have offset these costs in negotiating the property's purchase, but you will want to, or in certain areas will be obliged to, undertake this work. Similarly, termite or other wood-boring insect infestation may have been declared, but not treated, or subsequently become apparent, and it will have to be dealt with.

◆ Installation of shutters and alarm systems.

◆ Reviewing the electrical, heating and plumbing systems.

Properties advertised *prévoir travaux* involve major, more costly work such as conversions and complete transformation and redesign (described in Chapter 8) or restoration (see Chapter 10) and often require completion of the *travaux* before they become *habitable* – perhaps for the first time.

ROOFING

Roof pitches and regional tiling styles impose restrictions when renovating or restoring your roof. Making sure the roof is watertight, under the tiles, should not be confused with roof insulation (see 'Heating insulation and soundproofing' under 'Attics' in Chapter 7).

A sensible length ladder which means you don't have to put your feet on the last three or four rungs at the top, non-slip shoes in good condition, a good head for heights and a sense of balance are **essential** for DIY people. **Always** have at least three points of contact on the rungs: two hands and one foot, or two feet and one hand.

If guttering is non-existent or in poor shape this is the moment to put it up, assuming there are no local regulations to the contrary. PVC guttering and down-flow pipes are easily cut to length using a suitable saw and are fixed with a simple clamp screw system to the roof tiles. Water running off the roof should be caught and channelled into the guttering by zinc strips fitted under, and protruding from, the watertight roof layer described in the next paragraph.

There may be no watertight roof layer under the tiles in old properties. Chipboard panels (*panneaux de particules*) should be nailed to the rafters so that a level surface is obtained, onto which bituminous felt rolls or polyethylene rolls are nailed, providing this protection. A gap of at least 2 cm must be left between this layer and the subsequent tiling level for aeration, unless you are laying bitumen **roof** tiles (*bardeaux bitumeux*) onto bituminous felt rolls.

With roof pitches of over 30° bituminous felt rolls should be laid horizontally, starting along the bottom of the roof. Below 30°, unroll and lay vertically. The great advantage of bituminous felt is that it can and should be overlapped when laid, reinforcing the waterproofing. A 10 cm overlap is normal. Increase this if the roof pitch is particularly slight as rain water will drain off less easily.

There are bituminous roof tiles for houses and a separate variety for garages and non-*habitable* outhouses. Bituminous house roof tiles are economical and light in weight: ideal for residential mountain chalets with high roof pitches in heavy snowfall or heavy rainfall areas. As with horizontal laying of bitumen underlay felt, start laying tiles along the bottom of the roof. Special glue (*colle pour bardeaux bitumeux*) is applied to secure the tiles and the heat from the sun's rays strengthens adhesion.

In the South of France, renovation, replacement or restoration using traditional waterproofed **curved** terra cotta tiles is the norm. If the roof already has a watertight underlay and you don't need to change all your tiles you can either re-waterproof doubtful tiles or replace them with new 'old-looking' tiles. Cheap, nasty looking, plastic imitation terra cotta tiles also exist. Terra cotta **flat** tiles in various colours are characteristic of many regions, including Paris. New tiles are now mass-produced and cut to a variety of shapes and sizes, and they are slotted or nailed into place. Light-weight concrete tiles are an alternative.

Restoration of a slate (*ardoise*) roof with old slates is a specialist craftsman's job. As with terra cotta flat tiles, slates are now mass-produced and cut to standard sizes. They are fixed into place with iron fixing hooks. Quite attractive imitation slate tiles in aerated concrete (*fibres-ciment*) are a more economical alternative.

Strategic positioning of glass roof tiles (*tuiles en verre*) is a substitute for velux windows, especially if the space under the roof is for occasional use and not much light is required.

Useful vocabulary	
ardoise	slate
chèvron	rafter
colle pour bardeaux bitumeux	glue for bituminous tiles
galbé	rounded
gouttière	gutter
panneau de particules	chipbord panel
rouleau de feutre bitumeux	bituminous felt roll
toiture	roof/roofing
tuile en verre	glass (roof) tile
tuile plate	flat tile

TERMITES

The 'wood-boring insect infestation' law dates from 8 June 1999. It stipulates that the seller of a property, in a municipality that has been officially declared an infested area, must produce a certificate issued by a surveyor (*professionnel agréé*) dating less than three months before the completion date for the property's sale, indicating whether or not there is termite or other wood-boring insect infestation.

More than 3,000 towns and villages, in over half the French *départements*, are infected areas. These areas are the south-west, the Atlantic and Mediterranean coasts, the Rhone, Garonne and Loire river valleys and the Paris area. Most of Britanny and Normandy, central, northern and eastern areas of Frances are termite free. Consult the maps at www.termite.com.fr.

In the extremely unlikely event that no such certificate was produced when the sale was completed and you subsequently discover infestation (while you're up on the roof) **and can prove** through a surveyor's certificate that infestation existed before you bought the property, the previous owner will have to foot the bill for the expert's investigation. They will also have to pay for the eradication treatment, which must be carried out by a company with no links to the surveyor's practice. Best to insist on a *certificat d'état parasitaire* **before** completion.

If **you** discover a wood-boring insect problem in your property, in an officially concerned municipality or not, you must advise your town hall immediately by registered letter, on pain of being fined if you don't. A specialist company must be employed to treat the woodwork and ground immediately surrounding the property. Your town hall can advise you about this, but not normally on who to employ. Insecticides are injected into the ground, walls and wood, treating affected areas, and delayed action insecticides are also used to eliminate latent or potential problems.

A surveyor's investigation and report for a medium sized property of 100 m² with garden costs up to around €300. Treatment of the problem is rarely of great urgency so comparison of estimates should not be rushed: between €3,000 and €5,000 is about right for a property, with garden, of this size. Woodwork is guaranteed for 10 years and the ground and walls, five years. These are rather short guarantees considering the cost, so recommendations as to companies to use from satisfied people you know are more than useful.

Fungi growing on wood rafters is another, less serious, problem. Cut off the fungi and cut out parts of the wood affected. Refill the cut-out areas with wood filler and drill thin downward sloping holes into the wood so that you can squeeze in a wood treatment product. Then hammer in wooden plugs to re-block the holes and repaint or spray the wood with a restorative product.

Useful vocabulary

cheville	plug/pin/peg
état parasitaire	parasite situation
infestation xylophage	wood-boring insect infestation: woodworm
mastic à bois	wood filler

ASBESTOS

Asbestos has been forbidden as a building material for residences in France since 1997. Houses for sale whose planning permissions were granted before 1 July 1997 must now (since 1 September 2002) be investigated to see if asbestos was used in the construction, notably of walls, floors and ceilings or to insulate water and heating pipes.

Only architects or surveyors who have completed officially approved courses in asbestos detection are qualified to issue 'asbestos reports'. The asbestos report, indicating asbestos content and dust level or total absence of any asbestos, must be attached to the preliminary sales contract and above all to the property's sale completion document (*acte de vente définitive*). Asbestos dust level in the air (*niveau d'empoissièrement*) above five grains (*fibres*) per litre of air is officially unhealthy. However, there is no law at the moment obliging a house seller to neutralise or remove asbestos which gives off 'unhealthy' dust, although this will obviously bring down the sales price and may well dissuade the prospective purchaser altogether.

Houses being demolished, with the original planning permission granted before 1 July 1997, must also be investigated for asbestos. If you are employing a demolition company to demolish part or all of a property built before 1 July 1997, you must show the demolition company the architect or surveyor's asbestos report, which should also advise on remedial action to be taken for protection of the demolition workers if asbestos is present. These reports cost between €80 and €150 according to property size.

Don't overlook old garden sheds with asbestos roofing (see Chapter 11).

Useful vocabulary

abri jardin	garden shed
amiante	asbestos
désamiantage	elimination of asbestos materials
niveau d'empoissièrement	dust level (in the air)

LEAD-CONTENT PAINTS

The Préfet (the French government's *départemental* representative) can declare, as in the case of Paris where there are a lot of old buildings with high lead-content paint, a *département* to be a risk area for lead-poisoning (*saturnisme*). Houses for sale in such *départements* and built before 1 January 1948 must be subject to an expert's report which indicates *l'état d'accessibilité au plomb* (how accessible lead paint is to people). Children have a particular attraction for 'sugary' tasting paint flakes. The local town hall will advise you if its municipality is a risk area.

The law states that documents relating to a property sale meeting these criteria must include this report, at least one year old, at both preliminary and final contract stages. The seller has no obligation to renovate – stripping or painting over high-lead content paint with lead-free paint – unless a prefectorial order is served on them. This would be the case, for example, if instances of lead poisoning had been declared or if high probability existed.

As with asbestos, if the report is unfavourable an appropriate reduction in the sale price can be negotiated or you can withdraw from the sale using the seven-day cooling-off period (see under 'Buying' in Chapter 4).

You may want to have the property surveyed if it is post-1948, at your own expense, for lead-paint content before or after purchase to evaluate the amount of repainting required using modern lead-free paints. Reckon on €150 to €300 for a report, according to property size.

Useful vocabulary

état d'accessibilité au plomb	how accessible lead paint is (on property)
saturnisme	lead poisoning

SHUTTERS

Opening and closing shutters every day will probably be a new experience for you. Simple maintenance, like oiling the hinges and inside metal catches, is essential to keep them in good working order. The metallic support bars on recent (*maisons neuves*) shutters are rustproof, but check that they remain so. Panels of wooden shutters may, in time, warp or sag, which will make opening and closing them difficult.

As with doors and roof tiles, local styles and colour restrictions have to be taken into account if you need or want to replace shutters. Distinguished looking townhouses may have elegant louvered shutters (*volets persiennés lames arasées*) rather than shutters with vertical panels. The replacement style and colour must be uniform. It is advisable to have pull-down shutters (*volets roulants*), which leave no possible joins for crow-bar insertion, for street-level shutters as a security precaution – if you are in a townhouse with downstairs windows directly facing a busy pavement – and casement shutters (*volets à vantaux battants*) or louvered shutters upstairs. Metal burglar-proof bars can slide quickly into place and be fastened across double casement shutters (for double windows and French windows). Practical, when you're away.

Pull-down shutters can be fitted with electric 'up' and 'down' switches, remote control, cord-pull systems or manual winch systems. They may just have an 'up and down' handle. Tennis elbow sufferers are advised against using manual winch systems!

Security apart, how are the shutters going to be used? A sensible choice for a holiday home which is also let out for short periods would be hardy, middle of the range, easy-to-use shutters which require little maintenance. Presumably, you will take advantage of sunny periods: both casement shutters (if they are partially open) and pull-down shutters enable you to control sunlight streaming in. Sound and heat insulation are also factors to take into account.

Maintaining shutters

Although wooden shutters can last for years they do need to be re-painted (ideally, strip the paint back to the original wood preservative layer and re-treat) every two or three years. In windy coastal areas, however, this can be more frequent and unless you're lovingly restoring the wood, using wood filler, or really enjoy painting, replacement/renovation with PVC shuttering is an almost maintenance-free alternative

If you are sticking with wood don't regularly apply new coats of paint over old paint layers, as the build-up will eventually hamper opening and closing of shutters. The best way to paint is to take the shutters off their hinges and lay them on trestle tables. This also avoids continually mopping up paint drips with white spirit if you leave them hanging vertically on their hinges. Paint spray-guns accelerate the job, but you need a certain expertise to achieve an even finish. The average DIY person is better off with a suitable paint brush (not a roller).

Individual wood panels can be replaced in the case, for example, of swelling out, which indicates wood rot, and self-assembly kits for complete shutters are sold as well. To avoid future warping or sagging when you are buying new wooden shutters, look for shutters with three wooden battens forming a large Z-shaped reinforcement over the shutter's inside face. The reinforcement battens have a top and bottom screw plus a more central screw into each vertical panel. Untreated bare wood shutters can also be bought, which you will treat and paint yourself. Recycle the hinges and catches from the old shutters. Beech, oak, fir and exotic woods are commonly used for shutters. Buy locally to find the wood and quality most suited to your climatic conditions and if you are buying shutters that have already been painted make sure they have been treated with fungicide and insecticide.

PVC shutters cost more than wood shutters (around twice the price of fir wood shutters), but require little maintenance. Just wipe them clean, and keep the hinges and inside catches oiled. PVC is colour dyed thoroughly to avoid fading.

Perhaps you have a large property with the rear façade exposed to sea breezes and all the property's original shutters, which are wooden, need to be replaced. To maintain the original charm of wooden shutters, replace the façade and side shutters which do not face the sea with wooden shutters and install PVC where it really matters.

Before replacing all your shutters review your alarm system (see later in this chapter) or think about installing one. Check any special requirements in your household contents insurance policy as well.

Useful vocabulary	
affaissement	sagging
charnière	hinge
chêne	oak
espagnolle métallique	metal catch
hêtre	beech
peindre au pistolet	to spray-paint
pin	pine
sangle	cord-pull
sapin	fir
treuil	winch
volet	shutter
volets à vantaux battants	casement shutters
volets persiennes lames arasées	louvered shutters
volets roulants	pull-down/roll shutters

REVIEWING THE ELECTRICAL WIRING

Replacement of the main electrical circuit-breaker, the 'mains' (*disjoncteur de branchement*), if this is necessary, must be carried out by an electrician officially approved (*agrée*) by the EDF (*Eléctricité de France*). This national organisation has the monopoly for electrical supply to private households up to 1 July 2007, when the market will be open to other suppliers. 220 to 230 voltage, mono-phase is usual almost everywhere, but if 380 to 400 voltage tri-phase (three currents) with 30, 60 or 90 amperage is required, for example for a semi-industrial washing machine and tumble dryer combined, an EDF employee must adapt the mains.

Your electricity tariff

Check the tariff in operation for your household. Does it suit you, especially if you're not 'in residence' for certain periods throughout the year? There are two domestic tariffs. The *tarif bleu* has two possibilities: basic (*option base*) and off-peak (*option heures creuses*). With the off-peak tariff you have a choice of various reduced rate hours in the day or night. The *option tempo* is the other domestic tariff. It has several off-peak possibilities in a different number of days throughout the year. It is designed to lessen electricity demand in extremely cold weather when overall demand is at its highest. (Cold weather obviously means greater use of electrical heating appliances, but the prolonged heat-wave in France in the summer of 2003, which seems set to repeat itself regularly, also put an exceptional strain on the national grid system. The Minister for the Environment even asked householders to economise on use of electrical ventilation and air-conditioning systems.) The local EDF/GDF office will give you details of all tariffs on request.

Electrical circuits

A comprehensive modern electrical installation should have separate electrical circuits, each with circuit-breakers for:

◆ plug points (more than one circuit)

◆ light switches (more than one circuit)

◆ washing machine and dishwasher circuit (or one for each)

◆ water heating circuit (ideally, with a separate circuit for the bathroom or shower room)

◆ cooking appliances

◆ electric heating appliances

and a separate circuit for bathroom/shower lighting.

No electrical circuit should be used for more than five power points or for more than five switches. In a medium-sized three bedroom house, for example, three separate circuits for a normal level of lighting are usual.

Socket amperages and numbers

Generally recommended plug point amperages per room are: 16A for living rooms and bedrooms; 16A for the kitchen (with 32A for the cooker or hob and up to 20A for a separate oven); and 16A for other rooms (with 16A for a washing machine).

The norm in newly built houses is five plug sockets for the lounge and living room, three each for the bedrooms, up to seven or eight in the kitchen (including the cooker and washing machine) and one or two in the bathroom, not forgetting one each for the garage and entrance hall, and, if applicable, at least one for the basement or cellar. If your renovation requires planning permission (*permis de construire*) these norms, which are part of the NF C 15-100 electricity norm, must be respected.

Old properties are rarely up to this specification and they may need additional lighting even if you're replacing or enlarging windows – particularly large old country properties which often have larger rooms than newer detached rural properties.

French plugs

Change any UK three-point plugs on your household appliances to the round two-pronged French model with a female earth socket forming the third connection point; or buy some plug adapters before moving to France. High-powered appliances such as dishwashers and washing machines (*électromenager*) are earthed and large kitchen appliances, including cookers, are now installed with built-in wall plugs. **Don't** use a two-pin plug without an earth socket for an electrical appliance with three-core, earthed wiring. High-wattage lights like halogen lamps are also earthed.

To renew a modern sealed French plug on a French appliance, simply cut through the flex near the plug (once the appliance is disconnected from the power point!) discarding the old plug with the small portion of protruding flex, buy a new non-sealed plug, strip back a short length of flex and reconnect the wires to the plug terminals. If you're replacing an appliance's flex (and the interior wires) completely, note that wiring gauges (cross-section surface areas) for plug amperages are:

up to 15A	$1.5 \, mm^2$
16–20A	$2.5 \, mm^2$
21–32A	$4.0 \, mm^2$
33–38A	$6.0 \, mm^2$

Safety regulations

Key requirements of the NF C 15-100 electricity norm are: strict bathroom safety regulations; earthed plugs with special socket covers to protect children (and anyone else) from electric shocks; protective casing along the entire length of any flex which runs along interior walls from wall-mounted appliances and which is permanently connected (i.e. there are no plugs) to the wall socket; and an anti-lightning circuit-breaker if electricity is supplied by overhead cable.

The bathroom regulations permit:

◆ Low voltage lighting only (up to **12 volts**) in the **space over the bath**, if you have high ceilings, as it **must** be at least 2.50 m above the floor – with a switch at least 60 cm **outside** this space.

◆ **Outside the bath and above-the-bath area**, appliances such as electric razors, lights and heating units **which have dual insulation**. Look for product stickers with a square within a square symbol and a water splash within a triangle symbol.

◆ **At least 60 cm away from the outside edge of the bath or shower**, the theoretical idea being that you cannot touch them while you are standing with wet feet in the bath, appliances such as washing machines, which are **insulated and earthed**.

Once past the mains in the interior of your house you are entitled, in theory, even as a non-professional, to undertake any electrical work provided that the existing power supply is adequate. Obtain prior approval and technical and safety advice from an EDF technician. There may be an obligation to up grade your mains. **If in doubt don't tackle any modifications, extensions or replacement of worn out or out-of-date installations yourself**. The standard two-year guarantee (*garantie biennale*) covers electrical installation work by a professional company or person. The manufacturer's guarantee covers the appliances. The CONSUEL organisation (www. consuel.com) will inspect your installation afterwards, if you wish, and issue a certificate of conformity (*attestation de conformité*). The current charge (end of 2003) for private, i.e. non-business, premises, is €99.50; and €147 for a return visit to verify that appliances/installations conform if they did not on the first visit.

Re-wiring and updating appliances

Properties with wiring going back 20 years or more often have appliances that are not functioning correctly and which therefore need to be replaced. Before replacing the appliance and possibly adding another new one to an old installation, consider replacing the whole system to NF C 15-100 norms. Moreover, old wiring often has power point amperages unsuitable for modern conveniences, and the EDF tariff (see page 101) which would suit you best cannot be used. Some old properties may even still be on the old 110 to 120 voltage system, in which case a special transformer supplied and installed by the EDF for the use of modern 240 volt appliances will be necessary. When buying new appliances check that they have the NF (*Norme Française*) sticker or label which has a blue oval outline.

Useful vocabulary

attestation de conformité	conformity certificate
canicule	heat-wave
disjoncteur de branchement	electrical circuit-breaker
électromenager	household electrical appliances
gaine	casing
interrupteur	switch
option heures creuses	off-peak hours option
prise de terre	earthed plug

HEATING OPTIONS

Electrical heating

Although electricity is relatively cheap in France by comparison with many other European countries, it is not necessarily the best solution for your heating, cooking and hot water requirements. Consideration of the advantages and disadvantages of oil, gas and solar heating systems follow later in this chapter.

An example of an estimate (*devis*) for installation of electrical heating is given below, showing you the type of information it should contain. Prices are not indicated in the estimate, but an indication of appliance prices is given in the following paragraph. This estimate should follow an inspection of the property by an electrician to verify the existing heating insulation of the property in order to correctly evaluate your requirements. See also the section about estimates in Chapter 16.

Estimate for electrical heating (*Devis*)

Electricien name and address	Town and date
Company registration number (*N° Siret*)	Your name and address
Devis gratuit (free estimate)	

Main d'oeuvre (labour)

Calculation of electrical power needed for radiant heaters (*panneaux rayonnants*) and convectors (*convecteurs*); removal of old heaters including their wall supports; fitting new heaters including one with a time switch (*programmateur*); connection by a *fil pilote* of the different heating appliances to the radiant heaters with the time switch; wiring up to the connection box; checking that the circuit-breaker(s) functions correctly; testing and demonstration of the new system (*mise en fonctionnement et démonstration*).

Price per hour, excluding TVA: . . . . xxx€ HT × xx hours (*heures*)

Total main d'oeuvre . . . . xxx€ HT

Fournitures (appliances and sundries)

Lounge and living room: installation of two radiant heaters (reference name and catalogue number), wattage and dimensions.

Rayonnants, genre (type) *inertie*: these are wall-mounted modern cast-iron radiators which conserve and radiate heat **immediately**. (Not unlike larger floor-standing storage heaters which, however, conserve heat **overnight**.) . . . . xxx€ × 2 = xxx€ HT

Kitchen: installation of a 1000 W radiant heater (reference name and catalogue number), dimensions . . . . xxx€ HT

Time switch for one of the living room storage heaters with two programmes (*programmation 2 zones*) . . . . xxx€ HT

Bedrooms: one convector, 1000 W, in each of the three bedrooms (reference name and catalogue number), dimensions, colour. Electronic settings: Off (*Arrêt*), Comfort (*Confort*), Economy (*Eco*), Time switch (*Prog*) . . . . xxx€ × 3 = xxx€ HT

Bathroom: one heated towel rail, dimensions, catalogue name and reference
number . . . . xxx€ HT

Sundries . . . . xxx€ HT

Total (appliances and sundries) . . . . xxx€ HT

Total labour plus appliances and sundries . . . . xxx€ HT
TVA (5.5%) . . . . xxx€
Total TTC (inclusive of TVA) . . . . xxx€

If the delivery and work completion dates are not mentioned on the
estimate, make sure they are stipulated on the order form that is signed by
you and the company.

A reasonable hourly labour rate is around €30 an hour, HT. Nine to ten
hours total work including the preliminary visit would be about right for the
above installation. The appliances specified each cost: Soleido Applimo
radiant heaters, €700 HT approx.; kitchen radiant heaters, around €400 HT;
convectors, around €120 HT; time switch (*programmateur*), around €300
HT, and large heated towel rail, around €400 HT. A total TTC price would
be around €3,000. Aluminium is a particularly effective heat conductor.
TVA is only 5.5 per cent on the installation and materials, provided
everything is supplied, and the work undertaken, by the same company. This
applies to main and second homes which are more than two years old and to
all forms of heating (oil, gas, wood, etc.) provided the appliances are a fixed
installation. Mobile, plug-in radiators and radiant electric fires, for example,
have a 19.6 per cent TVA rate.

Useful vocabulary	
fil	wire
fioul (or) *fuel domestique*	heating oil
panneau rayonnant	radiant heater
programmateur	time switch

Gas central heating
Bills are about 20 per cent cheaper for *chauffage centrale au gaz* than for
electric central heating for domestic usage (heating, hot water and cooking)

using town gas. The latest gas-fired boilers reduce energy consumption by up to 30 per cent compared to old models. They are fairly expensive and do of course require annual maintenance, for which there are reasonably priced contracts (€100 is average), to ensure maximum efficiency. It is estimated that gas only becomes cheaper than electricity after 10 years: once the higher installation cost has been totally offset.

Approximately 45 million people in France (75 per cent of the population) now use *gaz naturel* which has replaced what was known as 'town gas' (*gaz de ville*). However, many rural areas and even urban areas do not have *gaz naturel* laid on and a gas storage tank in the garden as the only feasible possibility deserves reflection. The GDF (*Gaz de France*) revises its tariffs, not necessarily increasing them, twice a year (in May and November). The price of a local phone call to 0 810 140 150 will put you in contact with a local GDF consultant. French speakers can also visit the website (www.gazdefrance.com) and click on 'Dolce Vita' for information of particular interest for private householders.

Oil-fired central heating

Annual running costs for *chauffage centrale au fioul* are around the same as for gas central heating as there are no standing charges (*abonnement*). Initial outlay (boiler, hot water tank, pipe-laying, radiators and above-the-ground oil storage tank) is high and annual maintenance contracts average around €150.

Oil central heating offers evenly maintained temperatures and is a good alternative to gas if the latter is not available. Annual running costs are cheaper than using electricity for heating and hot water although you will still need to cook using electricity.

Under-floor heating

The Romans knew a thing or two! Both hot and cold air systems now exist with *chauffage par le plancher*. Re-flooring is necessary, using tiles ideally. Under-floor heating should not really be considered, therefore, if you're not re-flooring anyway. The most adaptable system is a two-way heating pump (*pompe à chaleur reversible*) blowing hot or cold air through a network of tubes set in concrete. Specialist installers are essential to avoid any possible floor condensation problems. The initial outlay can be considerable, but the system is extremely economical to run. Invisible, silent comfort is provided and heat distributed equally throughout the room: an advantage over traditional air-conditioning systems. Dry air can be a side-effect of any air-conditioning system and installation of a simple humidifier is the solution. Under-floor heating means no wall radiators, heaters or convectors: extra wall space.

Log-burning fireplaces and stoves

Restoration or replacement of existing fireplaces in period or old town or country houses are treated in the next chapter.

The addition of a fireplace (*cheminée*) in the lounge, or a wood-burning stove (*poêle*) in another living room, as part of the renovation of the heating system in more recent properties, creates charm, character and a feeling of homeliness. It also makes sense when used as a between-seasons form of heating instead of the central heating and as supplementary heating in really cold spells. Without redesigning your roof you should first of all, if you don't have a chimney stack, check that your roof pitch is suitable for one. Enclosed ceramic-glass fronted fireplaces (*cheminée à foyer fermé*) are claimed to generate up to six times more heat, using considerably less wood, than a traditional open hearth fire! The heat transmission advantages of a cube-shaped fireplace, i.e. with ceramic-glass all round, in the middle of a large living room, are evident. Fireplaces in all sizes, designs and materials are available through heating specialists, who employ or sub-contract installers, and the manufacturer's specifications indicate the room volume for which each fireplace is designed.

Fireplaces are subjective purchases so you should not think in terms of quickly recuperating the cost through reduced heating bills. Prices start at around €3,000 for a quality *cheminée à foyer fermé*.

Replica wood-burning stoves start at around €800. Ceramic finished stoves conserve heat particularly well and diffuse it like radiators. The manufacturer's specifications will also indicate the room volume which the unit can heat. Don't forget to have dry log storage areas if you're buying wood in bulk.

If you don't have a chimney stack, and building one is not practicable, and you still want that cosy flame in the lounge in cold weather, attractive Dimplex electric heaters with a log-fire appearance cost around €200.

Solar power

Environmentally friendly with an inexhaustible supply, solar power (*energie solaire*) can provide up to 60 per cent of household requirements. Two basic types exist:

1. An all-year-round solar hot water system, providing between 50 and 70 per cent of total hot water requirements. Solar panels (*capteurs thermiques*) which are strong, maintenance-free and durable, ideally facing due south and set at a 45° angle, can be roof integrated or fixed to the ground, local regulations permitting. South-westerly or south-easterly settings are also possible. The trapped heat is conveyed through insulated piping to storage tanks (*ballons de stockage*), inside or outside the property, and installation must be done by specialists. This type of system will not heat the property.

2. A combined hot water and household heating system, also providing 230V AC current, through a transformer, for some lighting and electrical appliances. (Solar power can also be stored in batteries for electrical use.) A small property or a second home in a particularly sunny area, like the South of France, can be self sufficient for heating and hot water. In other regions both systems will require a separate and independently powered additional hot water tank. These additional hot water tanks can be automatically linked to the solar system or operated manually as required. Additional heating (*appareils d'appoint*) such as convectors and fireplaces will usually be required for the combined system. Under-floor heating systems are now often generated by solar power and limit the amount of *appareils d'appoint* required.

Although solar power, which in itself is free and renewable, saves gas, electricity and fuel, the material and installation costs, even if you qualify for subsidies, remain high. A **small** installation of 10 m² of solar panels supplying hot water and heating for around 70 m² habitable area costs up to €10,000. This amount excludes the cost of any additional hot water tank and heating appliances. Subsidies from the ADEME (the Environment Agency for Energy Control) go up to €3,000 if certain conditions are met, and you may qualify for income tax relief.

However, if cost is really not a consideration, and your completely isolated holiday chalet, hunting lodge or mountain hut is quite impracticable for connection to the EDF network, and a generator (*groupe électrogène*) is not part of your vocabulary, go to *Energies solaires* in the *Pages Jaunes*. If your French is good, consult 'Plan Soleil' on the ADEME website (www.ademe.fr/particuliers).

Useful vocabulary	
abonnement	standing charge
ballon de stockage	storage tank
capteurs thermiques	solar panels
chaudière	boiler
chauffage centrale au fioul	oil-fired central heating
chauffage centrale au gaz	gas central heating
chauffage par le plancher	under-floor heating
chauffe-eau	hot water tank
cheminée	fireplace
cheminée à foyer fermé	ceramic glass-fronted fireplace
energie solaire	solar power
groupe électrogène	generator
poêle	stove
pompe à chaleur reversible	hot and cold air heating pump

ALARM SYSTEMS

Modern alarm systems using pre-selected and confidentially coded radio wave frequencies guarantee total and permanent reliability as there is no connection to the electricity supply. A video entry-phone system linked to an electrically operated entrance gate is an initial precaution when you're at home, but when you're not . . . Most break-ins in France occur during the afternoon (when people are out) and not at night (when they're in and sleeping).

When buying a property, ascertain before signing the *compromis* whether the alarm system you have seen in the property is activated. Ask the seller to test it for you. This may need a little diplomatic persuasion.

If the system is a rented *télésurveillance* system (the monthly rental can be as much as €100) you can negotiate with the seller to take over the remaining period of their contract. The monthly rent pays for the 24 hour, seven days a week surveillance service at the security company's office. The equipment is fitted and supplied 'free'. In reality you pay for the surveillance service and hire the equipment. The *télésurveillance* system does, however, provide one of the best alarm systems. It is composed of a central electronic unit (*centrale*) which interprets information received from strategically placed infra-red beam or electro-magnetic intrusion detectors (*détecteurs de présence*) which set off eardrum-piercing alarm sirens coupled to flashing lights (*avertisseurs*), relaying the information by a telephone transmission unit (*transmetteur téléphonique*) to the *poste de commandement* or *PC* (the round-the-clock surveillance service). You, local friends or relatives are then contacted by phone by the *PC* as an initial check, before the police are contacted.

With prices starting around €1,200, a relatively inexpensive alternative is to **buy** a *centrale*, two or three *détecteurs de présence*, and the keyboard unit (*clavier*) for recording and tapping in the confidential entry and exit 'System ON' and 'System OFF' numbers. In a town centre location, opt for inside and outside sirens. In relatively secluded areas a *transmetteur téléphonique* directly linked to local friends and relatives is a better option. Each member of your household must also have a remote control unit to be able to turn the system off.

Practical advice from people who have already installed *détecteurs* is recommended for optimum positioning of equipment for intrusion coverage.

For example, avoid positioning them in direct sun-light (the infra-red detector reads a sudden temperature change as 'intrusion'), and not opposite large windows where your own dog or neighbours' cats can be detected outside if they pass by. Fit detectors at the correct angle in places, to the side of windows, giving good room coverage, opposite the upstairs side of basement trapdoors, and near or facing side and front door areas through which an intruder must access the property. (You can forget about the bathroom and WC, but protect those rooms which contain valuables.) Pay your phone bill on time, so you're not cut off from the *transmetteur téléphonique*, and keep a supply of appropriate batteries for the equipment. You can always add to and modify your installation.

Useful vocabulary

avertisseur	alarm siren
détecteur de présence	intrusion detector
télésurveillance	electronic surveillance linked to an office

THE PLUMBING SYSTEM

Getting a plumber (*plombier*) to look at a particular problem you have like a leak or a blockage is no easier than in the UK. The increased demand for the services of a professional since the introduction of the reduced TVA rate of 5.5 per cent has highlighted the lack of qualified plumbers in France.

Certain repairs, plumbing extensions to the existing installation and modifications using modern PVC and polyurethane piping which can be connected to the original metal pipes can be done by a good DIY person following suppliers' instructions. Cold welding (using a soft metallic paste which hardens) is a relatively recent technique which simplifies welding between metal pipes and also between certain metals and plastic based pipes or tubes. It is most frequently used for repair work (leaks, etc.). A summary of pipe and tube materials, their applications and materials that can be connected together is given at the end of this topic. A *rénovation* enquiry implying big business **will** get a plumber to visit the property.

If you're in a particularly hard water area such as certain parts of Provence and chalky areas like the Champagne area in northern France, limescale is a problem. The granite rock areas of Britanny and the Massif Central (southern central France) are soft water areas. Combined water softeners and purifiers (eliminating excessive lead content) units are available from around €200. They can be fitted under the sink, using copper tubing (*tubes de cuivre*) and require little maintenance apart from adding special salt pastilles every three months. Check the amount by which the water is softened as water which is too soft is not recommended for drinking or cooking. Extremely soft water can also corrode.

Water is supplied by your municipality or more often than not by one of the mega water supply companies like the Lyonnaise d'Eau at a standard pressure of around three bars. You can, if you wish, fit a pressure reduction gauge (*réducteur de pression avec compteur*) quite simply on the property's side of the water meter. Properties built in the last 20 years or so generally have the water meter on the road side of the property, for quick, no fuss water company readings. If you're in a hamlet or a small village, water may be electrically pumped through your inlet pipes at little cost from a local well. It will require regular checking to ensure it remains up to drinking standards (*potabilité*).

Water companies are progressively treating water to reduce lead content in household supplies following a European Community directive which has been ratified by France. However, all lead content household water pipes will have to be changed after 2013 to comply with the new European standards, so polyethylene pipes are now increasingly used to replace leaking metal pipes. The *plomb* will gradually disappear from *plomberie* (plumbing)!

Pipe and tubing materials most frequently used

Material	Application	Can connect with
Copper (rigid or flexible)	Inlet pipes to baths, basins, bidets, sinks, WCs (*appareils sanitaires*).	Copper, brass, lead, PVC tubes. Cold welding can be used.

Rubber flexible tubes sheathed in plaited stainless steel

Connections from rigid *cuivre* or PVC *pression* inlet pipes, to *appareils sanitaires*.

Copper, PVC *pression* tubes using screw connections.

PVC (fireproof, non-corrosive, no scale deposits; suits hot (80–100°C) and cold water)

Rigid, outlet (*évacuation*) pipes, replacing old metal pipes for basins and washing machines.

PVC pipes gluing pre-fabricated PVC couplers; copper tubes by cold welding.

PVC *pression*, with the advantages (above) of PVC

Will be increasingly used for pressurised water pipes to *appareils sanitaires*.

Flexible, rubber, steel-sheathed tubes using screw connection. For joining PVC *pression*, use special glue or heat fusion.

Polyethylene (semi-flexible)

Ideal for laying on water from the meter to house or for garden installation. **Not** for hot water.

Identical tubing using a copper coupler.

Draw up a plan specifying lengths (be generous to allow for wastage) for piping and tubes even if you're handing the job over to a plumber so that you both know that you have an idea of what is involved. If you are doing the job yourself get the pressure limitations for the respective pipes and tubes right and double check the interior and exterior diameter requirements. (A tube's inside and outside diameters of 10 mm and 12 mm are indicated thus: $\varnothing$ 10/12.)

A variety of similar connectors, coupling joints and transition fittings exist, but often without identical usage. While the packaging or shelf display indicates the precise application for each article, you or the store's sales assistant (*vendeur*) can still be mistaken. Many large stores have an exchange, refund or credit policy if you return the purchase of any article in its original unopened packaging within seven days. Ask, if there's no display sign about this.

Mains drainage system and septic tanks

As in any civilised country, the property must have a mains drainage system (*tout à l'égout*) which is connected through public drains to the community's sewerage system (*réseau collectif d'assainnissement*). In the unlikely event that the local authorities install public drains after your property's construction you have two years in which to be connected! You will still have to pay for the connection.

Exceptionally, if the connection work required is shown to be disproportionately onerous – the case with isolated rural properties – a 'private' septic tank (*fosse septique*) which functions satisfactorily will be accepted. An old property that has had a septic tank system for years, with a pre-filter (*préfiltre*) and underground sewage disposal system (*lit d'épandage sousterrain*) – all performing satisfactorily – would only be required to connect to public drains if the public drainage network subsequently extended to a 'connectable' distance from the property. The two year delay for connection would apply and the property owner would of course have to pay for the connection. Septic tank systems should be serviced about every four years. Installation of a septic tank system with pre-filter and underground sewage disposal system costs around €3,000 for a five-room property, with a tank capacity of at least 3 m², on a level plot of land and with normal soil permeability.

If you **voluntarily** decide to renew or modify the property's drainage system you are advised to contact the local authorities **before** undertaking any work. Rules, regulations and requirements tend to change.

Useful vocabulary

acier	steel
adoucisseur d'eau	water softener
appareil sanitaire	sanitary appliance (bath, sink, etc.)
cuivre	copper

eau potable	drinking water
fosse septique	septic tank
laiton	brass
lit d'épandage sousterrain	underground sewage disposal system
plomberie	plumbing
plombier	plumber
réducteur de pression avec compteur	pressure reduction gauge
réseau collectif d'assainnissement	community sewerage system
soudure à froid	cold welding
tartre	limescale
tout à l'égout	mains drainage

10

Restoration

A genuine period house is the classic property which poses fundamental restoration questions. Do you have the time, money and inclination to find original enamelware, fireplaces, floor and wall tiles, roof tiles, shutters, staircases, stones, wood beams and doors, etc? And also to find the craftspeople with the knowledge and techniques handed down over the generations to satisfactorily do the installation and joinery work? Or will you have to settle for a second-best, cheaper solution: that of buying replica materials?

Restoration in the above sense means replacement, if the original material is beyond repair or if some thoughtless previous owner got rid of it. Restoration can also mean repair. An old slate tiled roof in Britanny or Normandy has just a few damaged tiles. Can you find a tile cutter who knows how to split and cut slate to just the right size and thickness? Can you find a stone mason who can cut and lay the same stones for that old stone wall (*mur de pierres apparentes*), perhaps a load-bearing wall, which needs attention? It can also include refurbishment, giving things a bright, new look again, but not too new. Look under *Artisanat d'art* as well as under *Rénovations immobilières* in the *Pages Jaunes*. You're unlikely to find a British builder, even among those established in France for some time, who has much experience of local period restoration work.

If you've decided to look for the original 'genuine' article, look for companies under *Matériaux de construction anciens* in the *Pages Jaunes*. The addresses may also include those of demolition companies (*Démolition: enterprises*) **and** companies that manufacture replica material. Don't confuse these two. In general you will pay more buying from a real *matériaux de construction anciens* company, who will probably have cleaned up the material adding a little refurbishment, than buying an article 'as seen' (*en état*) in a demolition company's yard.

Before doing anything, investigate the possibilities in each category (original material, repairs/refurbishment, replicas), as a combination of all three, if it's done harmoniously, could be the best solution. Allow time for travelling as specialist companies are not necessarily on your door step. Some companies have websites (see Useful Websites). Start with repairs (by a skilled craftsperson) or refurbishment which should be cheaper than replacing original material, then replace with original material anything that cannot be repaired, and complete with replicas for original material that is difficult or impossible to find or for less important items.

ENAMELWARE

You're not modernising the kitchen or the bathroom, but want to do something about the chipped enamel farmhouse sink and lack-lustre pedestal bath. Companies like RENOVbAiN (41, rue Brancion, 75015 Paris) use high-pressure resin sprays which fill in enamel chips and revitalise enamel surfaces, with new colours or flambé finishes if you like. This process is quick, clean and perhaps cheaper than replacing a period piece – certainly easier – and guaranteed up to five years. A renovated bidet costs around €150 and a washbasin around €240, with new colouring approximately €40 in addition. Look under *Sanitaires: réparation d'émail* in the *Pages Jaunes*.

FIREPLACES

There are numerous manufacturers of stone fireplaces which do not look out of place if you have to replace the lounge fireplace in an old country farmhouse. Replacing a Louis XVI marble fireplace or getting it repaired is another matter. Consult *Antiquités* (*achat et vente*) display advertisements in the *Pages Jaunes* and look for *chéminées*. In the centre of the Loire valley châteaux area (an area as rich as any in France for authentic material) Legens Matériaux Anciens in Saint-Avertin specialise in period fireplaces and other period (*époque*) materials. They have an excellent English website (www.legens.com). Origines, in Houdan, the Yvelines *département* near Paris, are international auctioneers specialising in *matériaux anciens*, including fireplaces (www.origines.com).

Prices, of course, depend on condition, and the supply and demand state of the market. Before buying period articles or before bidding at auction, verify that a certificate of authenticity marked *époque* or *style* is available.

FLOOR TILES

A concentration of split or damaged tiles in a particular area suggests a floor strength problem which should be put right before re-laying replacement tiles. Don't throw the old tiles out. They may be of value to a dealer in old tiles (*récupérateur de carreaux anciens*) who will restore or repair them. You could also use them if you're planning to lay down a terrace (see Chapter 12). Be prepared for some hard work if you are going to re-use tiles that were laid on cement. Having got them up in one piece, or two if they are split, chip off residue cement on the sides and back. Waterproof terra cotta and sandstone tiles, after they have been wiped or brushed clean.

Authentic old replacement tiles, if you can find them, require a generous budget as, subject to continuous wear, they need to be of good quality: buying second-rate or slightly damaged tiles is a false economy. It is preferable to buy them already cleaned as cleaning them yourself – don't use detergents – is extremely hard work. The real article is recognised by its impressive thickness, at least 2 cm, and obviously old appearance.

Prices of authentic old tiles start at around €80 per m² for good quality, restored material. If replica tiles are your choice or only solution make sure the material for sale is at 'replica', and not 'authentic', prices.

WALL TILES

Wall tiles of period interest in old properties are more rare than floor tiles. The existing wall tiling is often white or black and white and not attractive.

Quality hand-made glazed earthenware (*faience émaillée*) tiles, seal-stamped on the back of each tile certifying origin, are produced by internationally reputed companies. Salerne tiles, for example, from Provence, for kitchen work-tops, breakfast tables and splash areas, or even entire walls, in bathrooms and kitchens can be supplied to your individual design and room plan measurements, to fit in with your property's style. The cost reflects the individual attention to your order, the manufacturer's reputation and the quality of the hand-production. Off-the-shelf 'aged' marble (*marbre vieilli*) tiles, in different colours and sizes, are another idea: from around €35 per m². For a rustic finish, embossed tiles (*carreaux bosselés*) cost around a third of the price of marble tiles and are available in pastel colours.

SHUTTERS

Replacing shutters is described in detail in Chapter 9. The LaPeyre company (www.lapeyre.fr) have a made-to-measure service respecting various regional styles if you just need to replace one or two shutters of unusual size.

STAIRCASES

Restoring or replacing 19th century staircases is easier than creating outside steps using old railway sleepers (see Languedoc-Roussillon in Chapter 2), but considerably more expensive. Up to €3,000 will buy you an authentic 19th century wooden staircase with iron railings in good condition, but does not include the installation cost. Dimensions, height and turn direction are more important than with installation of a modern (see Chapter 7) or replica staircase, as your find will usually not be made-to-measure. If it is not quite high enough, get your fitter to build a raised base on the floor below the first step or an additional step or half-step at the top of the flight.

Companies such as Biewech, 25 grande rue, 28410 Havelu (fax: + 44 2 37 82 12 49) specialise in replica staircases.

WOODEN DOORS AND CEILING BEAMS

Perhaps an original wooden door is beyond repair or you're trying to find an identical partner for the kitchen to accompany the superb ornate solid wood door that leads to the lounge. If you're lucky and find what you want, re-hanging it so it swings correctly is often a problem as time and temperature changes have usually warped it. Why not use a door like this for an improvised cupboard set into a niche wall area? If your mind is set, however, on that kitchen door, this is when it is worth the expense of commissioning a cabinet maker (*ébéniste*) who knows their doors to faithfully reproduce the model which you already have in the house. Specify whether a relatively inexpensive pine wood or more expensive oak or walnut wood is to be used.

Prices for old oak beams, 20 cm thick, start at around €30 per metre. Beams certified as being over 200 years old and fashioned by axe (*poutres taillées à l'herminette*) – before saws were used – will be the most costly.

Saw-mills offer the best prices for new beams, which will need to be treated, but beware of buying unhealthy greenish looking wood which could warp in time.

RAVALEMENT

If you don't have a stone or brick-built property you will probably have exterior walls of breeze-block construction with roughcast finish (*crépi*) over a waterproof coating (*enduit*) which gradually gets dirty over the years. In the Paris area and certain municipalities (check with your town hall) outside wall face-lifts (*ravalement*) are obligatory every 10 years. Even if there is no local regulation, the town hall – the Mayor – can order you to clean up your walls if they are judged to be below the required standard (*pas en état de propriété*). Don't forget to notify the town hall – see Chapter 5 – before you do clean them up, just in case you decide, unwisely, to change drastically their appearance and colour!

It is important, therefore, to employ a reputable company that will guarantee the work for 10 years. There has been a spate of small-time cold canvassing companies in recent years, touting for *ravalement* work. A below-standard wall can usually be seen from the street! Beware! The prices offered sound interesting for immediate work taking a few hours, but the companies are often not local (look at the van's registration plates) so enforcing a 10-year guarantee, assuming you're offered one, would be difficult.

DIY is not out of the question, but experiment on a small ground-level area first, such as the inside of your garden wall, to see if you're happy with the result. If you are, hire some scaffolding (*échafaudage*), making sure that the hiring company erect and dismantle the scaffolding, and a high-pressure water jet (*Karcher*) to wash away the ingrained dirt – not too much pressure, otherwise you will remove an unnecessary amount of *crépi* or even *enduit* which you will then have to replace.

Having cleaned the wall(s) you will then put on at least one coat of *crépi*. A large wall area is best treated with a simple hand-rotated sprayer (*tyrolienne*) which costs around €25. It can be hard work turning the handle, depending on the amount and consistency of the *crépi* loaded into the machine. Make up your own *crépi*: one part sand (*sable*), to either one part cement (*ciment*) or one part slaked limestone (*chaux*), adding water for the consistency required. If you're spraying directly onto the *enduit* undercoat, i.e. there is virtually no *crépi* left on the wall, three coats are recommended: the first vertically and then two 60° criss-cross coats, just allowing each coat to dry first, but not to harden. Goggles, gloves and overalls are recommended. Small wall areas can be *crépi* sprayed without a *tyrolienne*. Dip a broom with a sturdy handle into the mixture and shake the mixture onto the wall, blocking the broom handle with a horizontal barrier, so that the broom's head doesn't actually touch the wall.

Ready-mix (*prêt à l'emploi*) *crépi* is used for a more decorative roughcast finish and is applied with a special roller with holes in the sponge (*rouleau crépi*). Elaborate decorative patterns can be created by skilled craftspeople using a variety of tools.

Useful vocabulary

artisanat d'art	arts and crafts
avec sceau apposé	seal-stamped
carreaux bosselés	embossed tiles
chaux	slaked limestone
crépi	roughcast
crépi granité	pebbledash
échafaudage	scaffolding
en état	as seen
enduit	coating
époque	period
escalier (fabrication, installation)	stairs (manufacturers, fitters)
faience émaillée	glazed earthenware
louer	to hire
marbre vieilli	aged marble
marche (d'escalier)	step (stairs)
matériaux de construction anciens	old building materials
pierre reconstituée	multi-stone composition replica stone
pistolet à air comprimé (Karcher)	high-pressure, water jet gun
poutre	ceiling beam
poutre taillée à l'herminette	(very old) axe-hewn beam
réplique	reproduction
rouleau crépi	roller sponge for roughcast
section	cross-section width/gauge
tailleur de tuile en ardoise	slate tile cutter
'tyrolienne'	spray-gun for roughcast

11

Redecoration

A September 2003 French television report estimated that DIY redecoration saves approximately two thirds of the cost of using a professional painter and an interior decorator.

For a painter look for *artisan peintre*, and not *artistes peintres*, under *peintre*, *revêtements: entreprises* in the *Pages Jaunes*. For an interior decorator, look under *décorateurs*. A *décorateur*, advising on style, colour schemes and textures, should not be confused with an architect (*architecte*) whose role (see Chapter 8) is much wider. A *décorateur* starts work basically, where an architect finishes. A *décorateur* will usually have a diploma from an art college (*école des beaux-arts*).

Although painting and decorating techniques are the same if you're in the UK or France, you may find there is a wider choice of roughcast (*crépi*) coatings in France, some of which can be used for both inside and outside walls. If you're putting on a new coat of ready-mixed roughcast on an outside wall it is worth considering using some of it inside and vice-versa. Vinyl wallpapers with roughcast texture and which can be painted are also popular. Decorating materials and how best to apply them are discussed below.

USING AN *ARTISAN PEINTRE*

Perhaps your property requires redecorating throughout, and two or three rooms, like the lounge, dining room and kitchen, are more urgent than the other rooms. Why not employ an *artisan peintre* who will make a better and quicker job of the urgent rooms than you can manage? Have a look at how they work. You may also be able to negotiate a better price through them for some of the paints and papers you will be using yourself in the other rooms, than if you buy directly from the retailer. A professional painter will usually have a trade discount and a monthly account with his supplier. Although there will be no question of a guarantee for interior work, his work and the cost of the paints and wallpapers he supplies will only incur a TVA rate of 5.5 per cent. You will pay a TVA rate of 19.6 per cent if **you** buy these materials.

EMPLOYING A *DÉCORATEUR*

An interior decorator with a professional diploma will obviously charge more than one without, so make sure the ideas and training you are paying for are justified. Ask to look at their portfolio (*press-book*) if you can't actually visit any properties they have decorated. Basic advice is on shades of paint to use depending on whether you want spaciousness and brightness or a cosy, intimate atmosphere and, of course, the materials which are best adapted technically to the surfaces concerned and aesthetically for the appearance desired. In the Paris area, an interior decorator's charge might be around €1,600 for around two days' work (redecoration plan – including floor areas as well as ceilings and walls – and locating materials) for a job with a materials and labour budget of not more than €3,000: €4,600 in all.

Visiting *salons d'habitat* (home decoration and improvement exhibitions) gives you plenty of ideas and enables you to compare prices easily. If you've decided to do everything yourself and know what you want you can usually buy at reduced 'exhibition' prices. Keep an eye on your local press for dates and venues. Cities and large towns have one about once a year, or there may be home decoration stands as part of a more general Spring or Autumn Fair.

PREPARATION

Walls and ceilings to be redecorated must always be clean, dry, mildew free, smooth and free of cracks and holes. It also helps if they are completely level, particularly if you want to put up wood panelling (see below). After stripping off wallpapers or paints (also see below), level walls with skilful use of *enduit* undercoats, tackling areas bit by bit rather than applying extra *enduit* over a wide area in one go. Try a small area to begin with before deciding whether to continue yourself or call in a plasterer. Part of the character of a period or old property are these irregularities, and redecoration materials may have to adapt to the limits imposed by the building.

Wallpapers should be stripped off completely so that you can judge the condition of the bare wall. Scraping the paper off with a scraper on a brick or breeze-block wall is reasonably easy provided the plaster undercoat has been moistened. For plasterboard interior partition walls, which are more fragile, a steam stripper (*décolleuse à vapeur*) is recommended.

Paint stripping is less fun and the scraping work may need to be preceded or supplemented by dabbing on a chemical stripping agent to loosen up the paint. Air the room, wear protective gloves and protect your eyes. Alternatively use a hot-air-cum-scraper gun (*décapeur à air chaud*), which is extremely effective.

Check the surfaces for dampness (refer to 'Basements' in Chapter 4) and any cracks. Widen any cracks found with a triangular head scraper before inserting a screwdriver to see if they are superficial or deep. Fill in the cracks or holes with crack-filler (*enduit de rebouchage*) and smooth over with a small trowel. You can strengthen repairs by sticking special stretch binding (*calicot*) strips along cracks before the filler sets, especially if the cracks are long ones. Repair deep cracks that traverse brickwork with a plaster mix (*enduit au plâtre*), mixed with water, following the instructions given by the manufacturer.

MATERIALS

Undercoats and roughcast coatings for interiors

An *enduit* for levelling or waterproofing purposes may have been used to thoroughly prepare the surfaces for redecoration.

Specific undercoats are manufactured for application on different surfaces and for different decorative topcoat finishes. Prices vary. Application of an all-purpose undercoat (*sous-couche intérieure tous supports*) is a good idea as you may, the next time you decorate, wish to replace roughcast coating (*crépis*) – which can be stripped (*crépi intérieure décollable*) – with a flat painted finish. All-purpose undercoats cost round €45 for a 2.5 litre tin.

Many ready-mixed *crépis* are suitable for inside and outside use. Application with a roller sponge is recommended for interior walls. Professional high-pressure spray guns (if you can locate one for hire) apply the product more quickly, but you must check that the consistency of the ready-mix product is suitable for the gun (*projecteur*).

Thick, ready-to-use paints (*peintures à effet*) applied directly by roller can be worked while still wet, using a spiked roller, bristle or soft brush to create rustic, textured finishes – ideal for country houses. Other paints in this category give imitation cork, marble, etc. finishes as soon as they are applied.

Cork, wood-panel strips and made-up wood slabs

Cork (*liège*) is particularly good for sound-proofing – a sensible material if your children want to transform their bedrooms or part of the basement into a discothèque. There are three basic types:

◆ natural cork (best for sound-proofing), supplied in sheets or tile form

◆ made-up cork (*reconstitué*), often with a vinyl outer coating – a mixture of natural and chipboard cork – and cheaper than 100 per cent natural cork

◆ thick (at least 20 mm) compressed cork slabs with rustic appearance –
ideal for farmhouse properties.

Solid wood-panel strips (*lambris*) are supplied bare (*brut*), dyed (*teintés*),
stained (*lasurés*) or varnished (*vernis*), while made-up wood slabs (*panneaux
plaqués*) are usually available in the form of a real wood layer over
chipboard or vinyl imitation wood wallpaper stuck onto multiply plywood.
Lambris are fixed vertically by nailing or stapling onto vertical wooden wall
battens which have been plumb-line checked. *Panneaux plaqués* can also be
fitted onto battens or, if the wall drop and surface is completely flat and
vertical, stuck directly onto the wall.

Paints
The principal types of paints (peintures) are:

◆ **White-spirit based paints** (*peintures glycéropthaliques 'glycéro'*). These
have a gloss or satin finish, take longer to dry than acrylic paints, are
highly washable and are extremely colour-fast. Polyurethane paints are
similar.

◆ **Water-based acrylic paints** (*peintures acryliques*). These have a smooth
matt finish, dry quickly, are not wash-resistant and will fade in time.

◆ **Vinyl paints** (*peintures vinyliques*). These have a matt finish, dry quickly,
are not wash-resistant and are not waterproof.

◆ **Water gloss paint** (*peinture brillante à l'eau*). These have gloss finish, dry
quickly, are washable, but yellow in time.

Matt and satin finish paints are particularly suitable for living rooms and
bedrooms: satin finish on wood is easy to wipe or wash down. Gloss paints
are better for bathrooms, laundry rooms, shower rooms, etc. Mosquitoes
(*moustiques*) and other insects are a nuisance in some areas, particularly in
the summer. Ask for insecticide paints if you can't find them.

This may be the moment to renew your paintbrushes. Packs of assorted
brushes containing a comprehensive selection of rounded brushes (for

angles, corners and fine edges) and flat brushes (for straightforward areas) are sold in large stores for around €15. Various types of rollers exist, including ones designed for applying varnish to wood, painting along moulded cornices, plastic ones for gloss paints and flocked (relief patterned) foam ones (*rouleaux à mousse floquée*) for painting wallpaper. There are others. Check the type of surface you are painting and the finish required.

Wallpaper and wall fabrics
An effective and easily applied alternative to an *enduit* undercoat (see above) **before** hanging wallpaper or a wall fabric – or applying a coat of paint – is the use of stretch rolls of fibreglass cloth (*revêtement toile de verre*). These rolls should not be confused with classic insulating fibreglass for wall and ceiling insulation. *Revêtement toile de verre* is stuck to walls and ceilings using special glue. Its elasticity means that surface cracks will not appear and any existing ones are contained. It is rot-proof and particularly favoured by painters and decorators for ceiling use in old properties. Generally 25 × 1 m rolls, for both walls and ceilings, sell from around €30.

Wallpapers (*papier peint*) are broadly classified as vinyl-covered (*vinyl*) and non-vinyl. The latter include white wallpapers with a roughcast or relief finish (*papier peint à peindre*, *blanc effet crépi* or *papier peint à peindre ingrain relief*) to be painted the colour of your choice. These are considerably cheaper than vinyl, but the cost of paint has to be taken into account.

Pre-pasted papers (*préencollé*) exist in both categories. They take a lot of sweat out of the preparation of the paper, but for ceilings – if you're ambitious – and porous plaster surfaces you will still need to coat the papers with wallpaper paste in the usual way. A special paste is necessary if you are wallpapering a gloss surface. Painted wallpaper for ceilings that are in far from perfect condition will result in a better looking finish than brush painting the undercoat or *revêtement* directly. Heavy vinyl papers are not a good idea for ceilings.

Vinyl papers are ideal for bathrooms and kitchens and there are also papers with good fire-resistant qualities. Although vinyl papers are washable, beware of relief patterns which may be difficult to clean properly.

Metallic dyed wallpapers (*papiers métallisés*) give that ultra-modern look. Use a special cutting knife for straight edges and buy pre-pasted papers as any join errors and rough handling show up easily. **Turn off the electricity before hanging** as this type of paper conducts electricity easily if it is moist.

If you want an illusion of a higher ceiling in an old village house use a velvety regency style paper with vertical stripes on the walls. For ceilings themselves, patterns should be light and discreet unless you want a psychedelic effect. Eye-catching wallpapers with scenic views are elegant if you have a large wall area which gives the impression you are looking at the real thing: they need to be hung and joined exactly.

Wall fabrics with foam backings (*tissu contrecollé*) and natural or synthetic fibre wall hangings (*tissu nu*) are, increasingly, an elegant alternative choice to wallpapers. *Tissu contrecollé* is around the same price as wallpaper. Synthetic fabric rolls with paper backing are a third possibility.

The hanging principle for *tissu nu* is like that for wood-panelling: stapling to pre-fixed wall battens. *Tissu contrecollé* rolls are simply unrolled horizontally and stuck, with a neoprene glue, directly onto a sound, smooth, crack-free wall. Synthetic fabric rolls are hung just like wallpaper.

No mess and relatively easy to hang or fix, wall fabrics can now be sponge cleaned and even washed or painted. Some are protected against stains in the manufacturing process.

Useful vocabulary	
artisan peintre	painter and decorator
calicot	elastic binding strip
crépi intérieure décollable	interior roughcast, can be stripped down
décapeur air chaud	hot-air-cum-scraper gun
décorateur	interior decorator
décolleuse à vapeur	steam (wallpaper) stripper
enduit de rebouchage	crack filler

enduit au plâtre	plaster (powder) mix
lasuré	stained
lessivable	washable
liège	cork
mousse	foam
papier peint à peindre préencollé	pre-pasted wallpaper – to be painted
peinture brillante	gloss paint
peinture à effet	heavy duty imitation finish paint
peintures glycéropthaliques	oil-based paints
revêtement toile de verre	stretch rolls of fibreglass cloth
sous-couche universelle/intérieure tous supports	all-purpose undercoat
tapisser	to wallpaper
tapisserie	wallpaper (noun)
tasseau	batten
tissu contrecollé	foam-backed cloth

12

Outhouses, Swimming Pools and Terraces

Outdoor improvements and constructions are still subject to the building regulations set out in Chapter 5. Windy and/or sunny situations, if you're putting in or replacing windows in an outbuilding or annexe, and seclusion or open views for a new terrace or swimming pool, are important factors among many others to consider before you start any work.

OUTHOUSES

Strictly speaking, *dépendances* means outhouses and outbuildings, stone sheds, barns, etc. which are actually independent of (away from) the main property. *Batiments annexes* are, as implied, storerooms, old garages or any other rooms which are linked to or an extension of the main property with or without communicating doors. None are *surfaces habitables*. So be careful you're not paying a hidden price for them in the overall price for the property which suggests they are considered to be accommodation areas. A property description with *dépendances/bâtiments annexes aménageables* signifies that the sellers have valued their property correctly. Wood or metal purpose-built garden sheds (*abris de jardin*) are not *dépendances* or *bâtiments annexes*, although large ones, at least 3 × 3 m, can be fitted out as summer kitchens (*cuisines d'été*) for quickly prepared meals in the garden.

Stone shed outhouses

Stone shed outhouses in the garden are relatively easily and inexpensively converted to pool-houses for a swimming pool's filtration pump and cleaning materials, summer kitchens with sinks and hotplates working off bottled gas, or a barbecue, games rooms or occasional summer bedrooms.

Remove any asbestos roofing and destroy it correctly. Long-life replacement roofing materials are cement fibre (*fibro ciment*), PVC or polycarbonate supplied in corrugated sheets. Allow for overlaps in corrugated material when screwing the sheets onto the roof battens. Honeycomb-form translucent sheeting, usually in polycarbonate, is an alternative to completely transparent materials. Polyester and polycarbonate materials have the best guarantees, up to 10 years, and other materials up to five years.

Larger outhouses

Larger barn outhouses and *batiments annexes* are more suitable for conversion to permanent living accommodation. The foundations should correspond to the anti-frost depth norms (see 'Foundations' in Chapter 6) and be in good condition. Investigate prices for any foundation work required before going ahead with your conversion plan.

Batiments annexes conversions can provide an opportunity to create extremely bright, high-ceilinged living areas. Eliminate ceiling joists and flooring of what was a loft area and install large polycarbonate roof panels, which have a solar heating effect, or velux windows. Complete, on a south-facing wall, with sliding picture windows which open onto an existing or planned terrace.

A garden barn can provide you with a self-contained bungalow or two studio apartments, providing you with regular additional income in holiday periods. You will not have to register as a business if the weekly letting periods total not more than 12 weeks annually (see Chapter 1).

Heating, roofing, checking for dampness, insulation and suggested layouts for kitchens and bathrooms if space is tight have been covered in detail in previous chapters. Studio apartments which are only used for holiday letting will not require investment in a central heating system. Individually operated electric convectors and radiators will do, supplemented by oil or odourless paraffin stoves, night storage heaters or a powerful electric radiator if you let in the winter holiday periods. The apartments should be well aired when they are not occupied and when the heaters are off. For a small bungalow which is lived in all year round you will probably need central heating, with additional heating from a centrally situated fireplace for extremely cold periods.

You may not be obliged to do up (*ravaler*) the annexe building's walls, but this **is** the time to do so, giving your additional accommodation a clean, fresh look.

SWIMMING POOLS

Manufacturers claim that around 45,000 private swimming pools are installed annually in France and the market's growing. This figure does not take into account self-assembly above-the-ground pools that can be bought from hypermarkets and probably does not include Internet online purchases of pool shells which are sunk flush to the ground.

The following factors should all be taken into account before choosing a pool or deciding, perhaps, to do without:

◆ utility
◆ position
◆ size
◆ safety
◆ construction type and guarantee
◆ cost and value

◆ appearance

◆ maintenance

Utility

Summers are getting hotter and longer. British coastal water swimmers, used to water 6 or 7°C (12 or 14°F) colder, should be able to swim on most days in outside unheated pools throughout the months of June, July and August in the southern France sunny regions (the Midi) and in many areas with continental climates. Covering a pool with a sliding PVC roof under which you can swim costs about another 50 per cent of the price of the pool, but with the water temperature increased by approximately 7°C you can enjoy swimming in May and September as well. Temperatures are hotter as a rule inland. If you like swimming, not just cooling off under the shower, and you live inland or want to avoid crowded beaches during the day, especially in the peak period from mid-July to the end of August, a swimming pool is a boon.

Manufacturers offer finance plans to spread the purchase cost because the outlay is important. But why not experiment for one year initially, especially if you've never had your own pool before, with a simple self-assembly pool with integrated filter? Prices and models vary tremendously. Carrefour hypermarkets offer, for example, a semi-rigid steel-frame, steel shell pool which you can actually swim in – diameter 4.50 m and depth 1.20 m – for €600 with a two-year guarantee. Smaller, inflatable lounging pools are cheaper.

Position

The ideal position if you have a medium sized property with up to 1,000 m² of land is facing south, away from overhanging trees (pine needles are a real pain), catching the sun all day so that the water is warm enough from around mid-morning, adjacent to a terrace so that you can dry off and keep your feet clean before going into the house and of course not overlooked by curious neighbours or passers-by. A large plot of over one acre enables you to build your own swimming pool complex (pool and pool-house) which can be away from the house. If the front garden is the only suitable garden space available you may encounter underground electricity and telephone cables or gas and water pipes. Check where they are. Some excellent above-the-ground pools are manufactured for long-term installation, and do not require a concrete base, so you can get round (or over) this type of problem. Above-the-ground pools supplied in flat-pack form are the only pools possible in rear gardens of terraced houses unless you are end-of-terrace or have an entrance at the end of the garden.

Size

Good-sized pools are rectangular rather than circular, from 8 × 4 m upwards. It's easier to swim up and down rather than round in circles! Double this area to allow for paved or flag-stone flopping out areas and allow a sensible splash distance between the pool and open French windows. A minimum distance of 3 m must be left between the pool edge and your next-door neighbour's boundary. The town hall will confirm the exact distance. Allow for a gradually sloping depth from around 1 m to 2 m, although a maximum depth of 1.50 m is sufficient unless you put in a springboard.

Safety

This is not a consideration. It is an obligation. Safety regulations passed in January 2003 stipulate that all pools installed in 2004 must be fenced in immediately to a height of 1.10 m, with existing pools in private properties complying with this regulation from the beginning of 2006. If you buy a property with an existing pool and rent out your property from time to time, presumably when you're not there, protective fencing must be installed immediately.

The exact height of 1.10 m may be revised upwards. (A peculiar anomaly is that the obligatory protective barrier or balustrade height on upstairs terraces or balconies is only 90 cm.) Check the situation at the time of property purchase or pool installation. If in doubt buy a higher fence, to be on the safe side. Fines for being on the wrong side of the law are heavy.

Construction type and guarantee

Most swimming pools over 20 years old are of *construction traditionnelle en dur*: concrete walled and bottomed with decorative stone walls.

PVC/polyester pre-fabricated shells or plastic-coated liners were in their infancy then and not as reliable as they are now.

Reinforced concrete (*béton armé*) pools are less likely to leak (they are also the most expensive) and a 10-year guarantee is the minimum period acceptable. With the *gunitage* process any shape of pool is possible as the concrete mix (*gunite*) is propelled through a pipe in a continuous flow following the outline of your excavation. It forms a single concrete block with no joins. Pools can be extended using *gunitage* at a later date if your family and friends out-grow the original pool.

Pre-fabricated PVC or polyester shells (*coques*) offer a comprehensive selection of shapes, sizes and depths with or without entrance steps: enough to suit most tastes. The shell is laid on a bed of sand in the excavation and will settle with the weight of water when the pool is filled. It is not advisable to change the water every season as this can disturb the shell's stability and even encourage it to rise off the sand. A 10-year guarantee is usual.

Single or double thickness plastic-coated liners are stretched over pre-fabricated wall blocks or thinner aluminium, galvanised steel, plastic or wood walls. All liner pools should have a concrete base under the liner. Concrete wall blocks with a thickness of around 20 cm are recommended in preference to the thinner alternatives. Single liners last around 10 years. Tears are difficult to repair with single thickness liners; double thickness liners (*liners armés*) are much more resistant and you can expect a 10-year guarantee – they should, in fact, last many more years. As with shell pools the pool should not be emptied after each season. The filter system (see below) will take care of day-to-day water cleanliness and natural evaporation will effectively result in all the water being replenished every two or three years.

Some technical terms
Aspirateur. Vacuum cleaner for the bottom of the pool.
Bache à bulles. Bubble-type plastic cover in contact with the water, which will help maintain its temperature and protect it from dust, diving insects and falling leaves. Also limits evaporation.

Doucine. Bevelled strip between pool sides and bottom which protects wear and tear of liners by smoothing the side-to-bottom angle.

Electrolyseur à sel. Programmed salt electrolysis cleaning system replacing the necessity to use chlorine and take a reading every few days. Takes the sting out of the water. Ideal, if you're not always there.

Filtre à sable. Sand filter. Water is pumped through fine sand and foreign matter is caught in the filter, keeping the water clear.

pH. The pH reading to show acidity levels is taken every two or three days in the swimming season with a liquid colour tester.

Robot nettoyeur. Mobile automatic cleaner/sweeper for the bottom of the pool, connected to the filtration system.

Tapis de sol. Protective underlay for use under liners of above-the-ground pools which do not need a concrete base.

Your mind is made up? Your swimming pool will make a good investment? The *Pages Jaunes* are flooded (!), see *Piscines (construction, entretien)*, with companies offering installation, maintenance and repairs *(dépannage)*. Talk with owners of the type of pool you're interested in and contact manufacturers of several years' standing who can also testify to several years' standing for their list of agents/concessionaires. If the manufacturer is local they probably sell and install pools on a direct sale basis to private properties.

Cost and value

Any pool that is considered to be a solid brick or concrete construction by the tax authorities – in practice most sunken pools – will be subject to property and probably occupancy taxation. (See 'Taxation' in Chapter 16.) As with fitted kitchens, value is immediately added to the property. Banks are therefore sympathetic to loan requests and will lend money at a better rate than finance companies suggested by swimming pool companies.

Bear in mind that the costs of excavation work *(terrassement)* and pool-surround tiling with edge tiles *(margelles)* and flag-stone slabs *(dalles)* should be added to swimming pool estimates. Compulsory perimeter fencing will now be detailed in estimates, but a practical cover with a roll-on/roll-off automatic or hand-operated winch system *(bâche et enrouleur)* will be an optional extra.

Appearance

Overflow swimming pools (*piscines à débordement*), pools with separate Jacuzzis, water jets below or above the surface, wave effects, fountains etc. should be planned for at the design stage. A pool house and flag-stones for the paved surround area (*la plage*) can be added later. Pool-edge tiles must, of course, be laid immediately. Take care to buy the correctly angled inwards and outwards corner tiles if you have an L-shaped pool as opposed to an oblong or square pool where all the corner angles are inwards. Mosaic or marble tiled walls for a traditional reinforced-concrete pool undoubtedly give the most elegant appearance. Shells and liners tend to be matt blue or white: less attractive. Under-water lighting set into the top of the walls is both functional, for swimming on warm summer evenings, and luxurious.

If your swimming pool is set away from the house and terrace, a more natural, less sophisticated appearance to suit the surroundings is an alternative.

Maintenance

A smallish pool of 8×4 m with average water depth of 1.3 m requires approximately 46,000 litres of water and, depending on the amount of evaporation, will lose up to 15,000 litres a year.

Some pool owners estimate that investment in water treatment materials and equipment, water pumps, water consumption and future repairs (when the pool has to be emptied) cost annually around the price of a first-class week's holiday abroad: €700–800.

The basic structure of a pool in an old property may still be sound. You can, of course, do a preliminary check when the water's clean and clear with a snorkel mask, but anticipate the possibility of future repairs to the stonework, when the pool must be emptied.

TERRACES

You might be planning a sun terrace, a shaded terrace, or a mixture of the two. Perhaps one leading from the house to the pool and another one for peace and quiet and a superb view if the property is in an elevated position. Will the terrace be left open or do you plan to build a brick half-walled veranda on it?

The answers to these questions determine the depth and type of foundations required, whether particularly frost-proof tiles should be used and the design and shape of the tiles to blend in perhaps with the flag-stones surrounding a swimming pool. If you want a terrace offering both light and shade you could install awnings with canvas, which are effective screens against strong direct sunlight and at the same time shower-proof and thick enough to withstand light winds. Awnings are usually guaranteed five years. Make sure they open up past the edge of the terrace for total shade when it's needed. Good quality fold-up arms, which support the canvass or plastic, should be fitted about every five or six metres if the canvass opens out to about three metres. An 8 × 2.50 m terrace, for example, needs three support arms. An automatic winder will save your elbow. Virginia creeper, or similar, winding its way over a pergola on the terrace is more natural but less flexible as regards sun and shade options. It's also messier, with dropping leaves and insects. Matting, which can be rolled up or down over a pergola framework, is an alternative.

If you haven't got a garden tap nearby this is the time to get one plumbed in. Terraces need to be washed down from time to time.

Foundations
Preparing foundations correctly and tiling them should not be undertaken lightly. Professional advice is recommended before deciding whether to do the job yourself or not. Building a terrace is more complicated than laying interlocking paving stones (*pavés autobloquants*) on a bed of sand for a driveway or laying crazy-paving, similarly, for a path using flat slabs of free stone (*pierres de taille*).

Frost depth norms should be respected (see 'Foundations' in Chapter 6) if your terrace is likely to be transformed to a room extension or walled veranda later on. Once you have dug the trench, a polystyrene strip around 10 mm thick, to allow for heat expansion, should be secured along the wall of the house before you start to build the terrace. Wooden planks should then be pegged into position forming a framework around the trench wall, which will encompass the various layers of foundation materials. Large terraces require several of these frameworks to allow for heat expansion. The frameworks should be approximately every three metres, leaving small gaps of between 10 to 20 mm thick when the planks are removed.

The foundations are laid as follows:

1. Spread broken bricks or pebbles evenly along the bottom of the trench and pack down into position with the aid of a thin layer of sand and a solid flattening implement.

2. If the terrace has a surface area over 6 m^2 (most terraces) a metal-rod framework should then be placed between two layers of cement. Otherwise one layer of cement will do. Level off the wet cement immediately, without smoothing off, and allow for a slight downward slope for water drainage **away from** the property of approximately 2 cm for every metre. For example, a 3 m wide terrace should slope downwards approx. 6 cm.

3. Allow a few days for the concrete to dry thoroughly and then lay down tiles using a recommended cement glue (*ciment-colle pour carrelage extérieur*). Sandstone (*grès*) tiles, extremely frost resistant, are often used for terraces with cement foundations. Tiles should be at least 8mm thick and labelled *extérieur: passage intensif.*

4. Remove the wooden framework after three or four days.

Terraces under 20 m^2 that are definitely not going to be supporting any brick walls can be laid on a sand base. Wooden frameworks are not required and, depending on the type of soil, the foundations should be dug to a depth of between 25 and 40 cm. As no technical aptitude is required, a terrace of this size is within the scope of any fit person.

Once you have dug the trench, the procedure is as follows:

1. Spread broken bricks, rubble or pebbles evenly along the bottom to a depth of about 10 cm. Then pack them down.

2. Overlay a bed of sand, a few centimetres thick. Then pack it down. It is advisable for larger terraces, i.e. over 20 m², to then lay down a cement, gravel and sand mixture making a concrete base of around 12 cm deep and when dry to put down another sand bed of around 8 cm deep.

3. Granite slabs or cement slabs can then be laid directly onto either of these surfaces.

4. Brush a thin layer of sand over the slabs, working it well into the joints, and hose down to get the sand to seep down into the joints. Brush off excess when dry.

Allow for the usual downward slope of round 2cm per metre for drainage.

Square duckboards (*caillebotis*) or washed gravel (*gravier lavé*) can also be laid on sand foundations to give a simple finish to terraces. Exotic wood duckboards are cheaper than teak wood and equally hardwearing and rot-proof, while washed gravel which is simply raked over from time to time is cheaper than any tiles or paving stones.

Useful vocabulary	
abri de jardin	garden
bâtiment annexe	adjoining/adjacent building
cailloux	pebbles
coffrage	framework
coque	shell
dalle	flagstone
damer	to pack down
dépannage	repair
dépendance	outhouse/outbuilding
fer a béton	metal framework
fond	bottom
maçonnerie	stonework
margelle	pool edge tile
pavé	thick paving stone or cobble stone
piscine hors sol	above-the-ground swimming pool

piscine en kit/prêt à monter	self-assembly swimming pool
plage	tiled or paved area surrounding swimming pool
plaque ondulée	corrugated panel
stores	awnings
terrassement	excavation work
translucide	translucent

Part Three
Practical Advice

13

Basic Materials and Tools

For our purposes this covers maintenance, tools and repair products (*produits d'entretien*) which will be used from time to time. Maintenance of woodwork, tiles, paintwork, etc. is enjoyed or reluctantly done by most property owners themselves. It is a necessity so it's important to buy the right materials at the right price and nin the right quantities (to avoid unnecessary wastage . . . if the use-by date expires just after you've dipped into the last pot to finish the job).

The previous chapters investigated the merits of the various materials used in construction, restoration, renovation and redecoration. Pick the brain of any professional you employ for this work – after all you're paying for their time – for advice on the best maintenance products.

WHERE TO BUY DIY PRODUCTS

National hypermarket and DIY (*bricolage*) chains such as LeRoy Merlin and Castorama have a tremendous selection of products. On a smaller scale, Mr Bricolage and Weldom have supermarkets throughout France. These stores will not necessarily have the same branded product for exactly the same job, which may be one reason why they regularly offer to reimburse you the difference in price between their price and a cheaper price (if you find one) for the identical product elsewhere. They often have their 'own label' product, cheaper, but not necessarily better than another brand. These reimbursement offers also apply particularly to large tools and appliances. Other national DIY chains include Bricomarché, Gedimat (who also sell building materials) and Bricorama.

Regionally, there are local chains of builders' merchants (*marchands de matériaux*) and still some old-established independent family firms. Both these types of outlets trade a lot with professionals. They therefore offer good advice and will sell you the most suitable product. Tiling specialists, often independent companies, are found throughout France. Tiles are attractively wall, counter or floor displayed and you will generally obtain first class advice as to what tile to buy for what job and the best fixing glue or paste to use.

GENERAL MAINTENANCE

Fixing glues (*colles*) exist for general household use, glass, plastic and wood, as well as contact (*néoprene*) and instant-stick glues. These are not to be confused with wallpaper pastes and tiling cement mixes, which are also known as *colles*. Lubricants (*lubrifiants*) include penetrating oil (*dégrippants*) such as '3 in 1'. White spirit is found everywhere and is still called 'white spirit'.

Varnish products (*produits de vernissage*) are now largely used, replacing former wax products, to waterproof wood and keep it clean: ideal for half-timbered façades and parquet floors. Indoor and/or outside use is specified on the label. Note that some parquet panels are already treated by the manufacturer. Oil-based products are less resistant and are best used on woods such as teak which are naturally oily. Dirty wooden floors which have been waxed should be stripped down with a special de-waxing product (*décireur*) before being re-treated.

Newly laid floor or wall tiles usually have traces of excess cement or glue on the surface. Wall tiles can be cleaned with a sponge moistened with a water and white vinegar mixture. Sponge over several times, as necessary, wringing out the sponge frequently. For floors, wait until the tiles are completely dry – up to three or four months may be necessary depending on the rooms – and then wipe over with a slightly wet mop. Terra cotta tiles and earthenware (*faience*) tiles may need different additional treatment. Ask the supplier. Glue spots are removed with a benzene product, ink with alcohol, tar with benzol, oil-based paints with ethyl alcohol (*alcool méthylique*) and fruit stains with pure alcohol.

Apart from regular hoovering, carpets should be cleaned from time to time with a dry cleansing powder which is sprayed on (*bombes aérosols à mousse sèche*). Allow time after the product has penetrated the surface for it to be effective, before hoovering over. A shampooing machine (*shampouineuse*) can be hired for thorough cleaning every few years. Employ a specialist company to disinfect carpets completely if you develop an allergy, or consider re-laying the floor with tiling or parquet.

Don't forget to clean fireplaces and chimneys out regularly using *pré* or *après ramonage* (before or after chimney-sweeping) products. These salt-based products are used while the fire is burning to remove potentially inflammable tar stuck to the flue which cannot be brushed away.

Guttering should be cleared manually of leaves and moss removed from roof tiles, about once a year.

Annual maintenance contracts (*contrats d'entretien*) are recommended for gas boilers. Septic tank drainage systems should be cleaned by a specialist around every four years.

TOOLS

Tools fall into two categories: those to buy and those to hire.

Tools to buy include many you will already be familiar with for odd jobs round the house plus some more specialised ones for jobs you have decided to do for the first time. As well as the stores and builders' yards referred to above, tools can be bought in local hardware shops (*quincailleries*). Some enterprising out-of-town dealers have walk-in container size trucks which set up shop for the day in town parking areas. Look out also for practical demonstrations if you're not sure if the tool is designed for your job and also for closed circuit TV demonstrations in large stores. Electrical tools should be guaranteed for at least one year.

The vocabulary list below is not exhaustive, and assumes that you already have a few hammers (*marteaux*), hand-saws (for wood) (*scies égoines*) and screw drivers (*tournevis*).

Clamps and spanners

Clé à molette	Adjustable spanner
Clé à fourches	Open end spanner. Numbered progressively according to size.
Etabi pliant portable	Folding and portable work-bench
Etau	Vice
Pince	Pliers. There are various types.
Serre-joint	C-clamp

Cutting tools (*outils de découpe*)

Coupe carreaux	Tile cutters. Large range available. From around €15 for a small hand tool for interior tiles only, which are thinner than outside tiles. Check the tile thickness cutting limits. New outside tiles are at least 8 mm thick and older restored tiles are considerably more. Electric cutters are a solution if there are a pile of thick outside tiles to be cut precisely, but shop around as prices and qualities vary a lot.
Pince universelle	Multi-purpose electrician's tool, incorporating wire cutter (*coupe-fil*) and wire stripper (*denude-fil*).
Scie à métaux	Hacksaw. Ensure the saw is suitable if you're sawing plastic pipes for guttering.

Drills (*perceuses*)

Perceuse éléctrique	Electric drill. Look for battery operated ones (*sans fil*). Remember to use special screws for partition wall fixtures and keep within load-bearing limits if fitting wall units.
Chignole	Hand drill

Fixing tools (*outils d'assemblage*)

Mallet	Mallet
Tournevis cruciform	Crosshead screwdriver. Automatic or hand screwdrivers can be bought with interchangeable flat and cross-head blades.

Masonry tools (*outils de maçonnerie*)

Grattoir triangulaire	Triangular scraper. Used for scraping out plaster in cracks before making good.
Pistolet à calfeutrer	Caulking injection gun for silicon joints, grouting, etc. Sometimes sold with the filler.
Tire-joint	Joint filler
Truelle de maçon	Brick-layer's trowel
Truelle de plâtrier	Plasterer's square trowel. Can be used for applying plaster, roughcast, etc. A larger rectangular or square board with a handle (*taloche*) is then best used for removing excess and levelling off.

Drawing and measuring instruments

Equerre à talon	Set square
Fil à plomb	Plumb line
Mètre pliant	Folding measuring rule
Niveau à bulle	Spirit level

Paintwork

Grattoir	Scraper
Pistolet à peinture	Spray paint gun. Paint spraying requires a steady hand and the correct consistency in the paint mix. Experts produce quality finishes rapidly. DIY people

are advised to use a spray paint gun for rooms of secondary importance like converted attics and basements where perfection is not essential. Two coats should be sprayed: a horizontal one in a continuous zigzag, followed by a vertical one in a continuous zigzag , or vice-versa. Test an area to begin with.

Shaping, smoothing tools (*outils de façonnage*)

Ciseau à bois	Chisel
Lime	File
Ponceuse	Sander. Buy one adaptable for various grades of sandpaper.
Rabot	Plane

SPECIALISED EQUIPMENT

Expensive equipment that you are likely to use very occasionally, like cement mixers (*bétonnières*), high-pressure water spray guns (*Karcher nettoyeur à haute pression*) and motorised water pumps – if you suddenly have to empty around 45,000 litres of water from the swimming pool – can be hired on a daily basis.

Protective clothing, footwear, gloves, goggles and face masks should not be overlooked. Overalls which can get dirty and will not hinder you; goggles which you can wear over spectacles which won't distort your vision; non-slip boots or shoes, with stiff toes to avoid stubbing accidents, for ladders or slippery surfaces; and dust and face masks for carpentry work (when sawing wood or plasterboard materials), painting and decorating.

14

Companies, Materials and Shopping Around

Details of the principle seals of approval for building companies and their work, and for building materials, follow. Although work is subject to the standard two- or ten-year guarantees and you will have ensured that the company you use has appropriate insurance to cover any defective work, it is sensible, particularly where major construction work (foundations, walls or roofs, for example) is concerned, to take out your own insurance. This insurance will pay out immediately for urgent repairs before the responsibility for the defective work is officially attributed. This type of cover (*l'assurance dommages-ouvrage*) is most appropriate when there are several different companies (builders, carpenters, fitters, tilers, electricians, etc.) working on the same job, perhaps under an architect's supervision. An architect will be able to advise you and may recommend insurance companies.

BUILDING COMPANIES

Qualibat

Companies approved by Qualibat bear the distinctive blue and white pyramid logo on their headed paper. All types of building companies' work is covered except electrical (see **Qualifelec** further below). The Qualibat certificate of approval is issued to a company for five years by this independent organisation, acting in the interests of the maintenance of building work standards and customer satisfaction, after thorough investigation of the company's technical ability, administrative status, insurance cover and financial standing. Every year, during the five year period, a Qualibat approved company is obliged to update information in order to obtain a valid certificate for the year in question. The website www.qualibat.com can be consulted easily with a little basic French for a list of approved specialist companies in your area.

Maître Artisan

A distinctive red logo on a diamond shaped base is the chamber of trade's (*chambre de métiers*) seal of approval of a company's technical expertise. It is by no means issued automatically, and its acquisition indicates that the company has a high level of competence and that the boss of the company has 10 years' experience of their trade. The MAAF insurance company, in addition, awards a special vote of confidence to companies or individual builders that have a 10 year claim-free record.

If you're looking for an outstanding company choose one that has both Qualibat (or Qualifelec, see below) and Maître Artisan approval, but don't automatically reject a company recommended to you that has neither of these seals of approval. A number of competent companies don't bother to apply for these certificates.

Cheque Emploi Service

Some building professionals working by themselves offer the 'Cheque Emploi Service' system which means that **you** employ them for the total number of hours agreed as a salaried employee. Write to, phone or fax the Centre National du Chèque Emploi Service, 3, avenue Emile Loubet, 42961 Saint-Etienne cedex 9 (Tel: + 33 (0)4 77 43 23 50, Fax: + 33 (0) 4 77 43 23

79) for details. Banks issue the special cheque books with employer's declaration form to be completed when a payment is made.

The property must be your main residence and there is now up to €5,000 in annual tax relief if you pay income tax in France. Bear in mind that you pay the employer's and employee's social security contributions, by direct debit, totalling at least 55 per cent on top of the salary cheque. You will pay for the materials at the higher rate of VAT (19.6 per cent) so make sure your builder negotiates an adequate discount for you with the supplier. **The *Cheque Emploi Service* is a system only to be used if you have a strong recommendation regarding the reliability and competence of the builder.** While materials are subject to manufacturers' guarantees, the work is not subject to an official guarantee.

Qualifelec

Approved electrical installation companies have the blue-striped QE logo on their headed paper. It is similar to Qualibat criteria as regards technical competence. However, administrative standing, insurance cover and financial standing are not necessarily investigated. The Qualifelec certificate of approval is valid for three years. The website www.qualifelec.fr can be consulted easily as for Qualibat, with a little basic French, for a list of approved specialist companies in your area.

English-speaking companies

Embassies and consulates sometimes have lists of professional companies with English-speaking staff and there is now the website www.theanglophonebook.com: an online telephone directory, in English, of English-speaking businesses on the French Riviera.

BUILDING MATERIALS

NF products

Look for a white NF set in a blue ellipse logo. With a wide application, from bricks to taps, this is the French standards label guaranteeing quality. It also meets any obligatory European standards. Some products also have an 'environment friendly' label.

Certificats CSTBat

Recognised by the *CSTBat* logo. This certification, issued by the Scientific and Technical Building Industry centre (CSTB), follows examination and approval by an independent organisation of **new** techniques and products. While the product itself will have a first-class guarantee, you should obtain professional advice as to its suitability for your job. A specialist accustomed to the new techniques involved is best employed to carry out the work.

Acotherm

This is a special label indicating heat insulation and soundproof qualities on a points rating system for window units, provided, of course, that the windows are fitted correctly. Other labels indicating recognised standards of quality exist, such as **Upec** for floorings and **A2P** for alarm systems. Some products, like wood-burning fireplaces, have a performance rating label in addition to the **NF** standard denoting the approved construction quality. (The **NF** standard for fireplace quality and safety is NFD 35376 and the **Flamme Verte** logo with a flame symbol indicates that the fireplace heats effectively and is environmentally friendly.)

'Private labels'

These are also issued by groups of companies whose products are known to be manufactured to a certain standard and originating from one locality: rather like 'Champagne' on bottles of Champagne which certify that the drink originates from the Champagne area of France and has been produced in accordance with the traditional *méthode champenoise*. For example, if you want renowned Salernes wall or floor tiles most of the manufacturers in the Salernes area of Provence in the Var département now have a *'Terre de Salernes'* label for their products.

SHOPPING AROUND

Unless you're deep in the countryside you will have a good choice of retail stores (see Chapter 13) selling electrical tools and appliances, glass, hand tools, heating appliances, hardware, lighting, paints and wallpapers, plumbing material, floor and wall tiles and wood shelving, battens, panels, etc. within half an hour's drive. You may have to go a bit further for your local megastore, like Leroy Merlin or Castorama, which have all these items plus building materials – bricks, sand, cement mixes, flagstones, insulation panels – under the same roof.

Assuming that you are choosing the materials required yourself, rather than leaving this to a professional, take the time and trouble to physically inspect similar materials in different stores and then do comparative checks on the websites (see Useful Websites) for current prices, easy payment terms and promotional offers. Read the publicity in your letter box too (there's always plenty) to keep abreast of current offers. Some stores may offer three or four equal instalments charging no interest while others may offer up to 10 equal instalments for just an additional 1 per cent cost, subject to your credit worthiness. All national chains accept international credit cards and there are also company loyalty cards offering price advantages on a points-accumulated basis or deferred payment. In some building merchants' yards you can load your car or van directly from the materials storage area. If the material has to be delivered to your home don't forget to include the delivery cost or the reasonable van hire rates listed by the store in your overall calculations.

The websites also have buying advice for certain materials and installation tips and procedures for certain jobs. You will also find free brochures containing this information in large stores.

Every two years, at the end of October/early November, the International Building Materials and Technologies Trade Show (Batimat) takes place at the Porte de Versailles exhibition grounds in Paris. It is open to the trade and non-professionals, and the latest products and devices are displayed and demonstrated. The website address is: www.batimat.com (in French and English).

Useful vocabulary

assurance dommages-ouvrages	construction defect insurance
fiche technique de conseil	(small) instructional guide
guide d'achat	product information and advice buying guide
quatre fois sans frais	four interest-free instalments
sans frais	interest free

DIY, ARCHITECT OR PROFESSIONAL CONTRACTOR?

Do-it-yourself

DIY superstores are the third largest, in number, of category store outlets in France, after hypermarkets and supermarkets, and that does not take into account hypermarkets which have *bricolage* and *outillage* sections. It is estimated that almost one third of French property owners have a renovation or building project in mind, so you are not alone.

As we have seen, planning permission is not required where alterations, redecorations or improvements to the inside of an existing property do not change its functional status (from non-inhabitable to habitable), or if it is already habitable. DIY can be carried out for a lot of inside work which does not affect the basic structure of outside walls, inside load-bearing walls, roofs and upper floors, etc. of a property. Retailers supply sufficient information, practical advice and free instructional brochures to bring many jobs safely within the reach of the motivated amateur who has a basic command of French. Read the use and application instructions on the packaging carefully, particularly for products like paints and wall coatings, as more and more products have been developed for very specific uses. General purpose products are more and more rare. Make sure you get the most suitable product. Use the right tools and wear appropriate protective clothing and equipment. DIY accidents in France account for 5 per cent of accidents in the home.

Employing professionals

If planning permission is required a good rule of thumb is to employ professionals: an architect to draw up the plans clearly for an extension, to make sure the project is technically sound and to present the application for planning permission correctly; and qualified approved builders who will keep strictly to the plan and to building regulations. Extremely heavy fines, demolition or rectification work can be imposed if a local authority's inspection reveals that the work does not comply. Potential buyers of properties should ask to see the planning permission papers for structural changes that have been made to properties and the certificate of conformity **before** deciding whether to buy. A new property owner can be made to demolish any work that has been carried out illegally by the previous owner.

While it costs up to 12 per cent of the cost of the total job to employ an architect to produce an attractive blue-print, co-ordinate different building work and ensure that the project's time-table is respected, this amount may well be recuperated immediately through their buying expertise in negotiating prices with suppliers, builders and fitters. Not to mention the added value (*la plus-value*) that a sensible project will bring to the re-sale potential of the property. An ill conceived DIY plan can have the opposite result.

With VAT recently confirmed at only 5.5 per cent, up until the end of 2005, on most improvement (not construction) work carried out by professionals on properties over two years old, don't miss the opportunity to get a professional job done at the lowest possible cost and guaranteed for up to 10 years.

Restoration work may involve urgent major roofing and wall treatment work so that you can live in a dry property *hors d'eau* (literally 'out of the water') as quickly as possible. An architect supervising builders and keeping you regularly posted is essential, especially if you're not living nearby. Renovation work, on the other hand, may include the outside wall coatings and various interior improvements where urgency is not the key factor and you may already be in residence. In this case, while builders may still be essential, an architect is optional.

If finance is required (see the next chapter) from banks or other organisations, you will have to use professional contractors as estimates or invoices will be required.

15

Cost, Finance, VAT and Taxation

COST

Chapters 2, 3 and 4 gave you some indications of **property prices** and where to see properties advertised. The French website www.immoprix.com gives **average** prices for properties **sold** (new and old houses and also new and old apartments) over the previous year in towns and areas throughout France. The averages for new and old houses give average number of main rooms and average plot sizes.

Have two budgets for **work** on the property: one for immediate work, whether it's simple renovation or complete transformation, and the other for improvements that will come to mind after your initial blue-print has been completed. The immediate work usually costs more than predicted even if you've been able to obtain detailed and binding estimates before purchase of the property via, for example, a sole selling agent, so you will need to dip into your improvements budget. Unforeseeable technical problems may also be encountered and these will not necessarily be covered by the terms of your estimates.

Estimates

Three estimates, through recommendations, approved list builders or using an architect or the estate agent that has sold you the property, are always advised for major work (walls and roofing, new floor levels, bathroom, heating, kitchen installations, etc.). If one of the estimates is considerably lower than the other two, which are in close competition with each other, look closely at the materials specified. The quality of work may be sound in the lowest estimate but are the materials similar to those in the higher estimates and are they what you're really looking for? If the amounts of the three estimates are similar you will have an indication of the going rate for a good job with suitable materials.

Try to obtain free (*gratuit*) estimates. (The Lapeyre company, a first class supplier and installer of fittings and fixtures for the home, charge €50 for any visit to your home to measure up, but this is deducted from their invoice if you accept their estimate.) '*Gratuit*' should be indicated on the estimate, with its period of validity, delivery and work completion dates and payment terms. If there is a delay in delivery of more than seven days and the estimate exceeds €500 you are legally entitled to cancel your order, except if the company has a valid *force majeure* reason (fire, flooding, etc.). The same conditions apply if completion of the work itself is seven days over schedule, but it is difficult in practice to find and change workers halfway through an installation job. With the continuation of the reduced VAT rate of 5.5 per cent on most home improvement work you will be asked to sign a declaration (*attestation*), when you accept an estimate, stating that the property is more than 50 per cent residential and over two years old.

Architects often charge for their estimate of what their services will cost, if they do not apply a percentage rate to the overall cost of your project. In general, this charge will be deducted from their payment if they are retained.

The national association for kitchen equipment and fittings (*Le Syndicat National de l'Équipement de la Cuisine*) recommends a 25 per cent down payment for appliances and units when you order, followed by 65 per cent when the fitter arrives with all the material to start the installation, with the balance of 10 per cent on completion of the work; and for the labour, 25 per cent down payment with your order, 25 per cent when the fitting starts and the balance on completion. You may, however, have to settle for at least a 30 per cent down payment if the *cuisiniste* has to order your kitchen units from the factory. Some kitchen companies sub-contract the fitting work to a fitter who is not their salaried employee. In this case you may have nothing to pay for the fitting work until the job is completed. Make sure, however, that you will still pay VAT at the reduced rate of 5.5 per cent, and that the overall guarantee for the materials and installation is not affected.

There is no national association for bathroom equipment and fittings. A down payment of up to 50 per cent is usual when you accept an estimate, with the balance payable on completion of the installation which includes any floor and/or wall re-covering specified in the estimate. For construction work, such as an extension, it is usual to make stage payments up to completion of the work. Part of an architect's brief will be to advise you on payment releases subject to their inspection of the work's progress.

Prices for materials sold through outlets which deal mainly with the building trades are often spoken of exclusive of VAT (*hors TVA* or *HT*) as professionals are reimbursed VAT when they make their quarterly VAT returns. Allow for VAT (see 'VAT (TVA)' in this chapter) in your costing if you're buying through these suppliers. If you are a *louer en meublé professionnel* (see Chapter 1) with a regular requirement for materials you should qualify for discount on purchases through these outlets.

FINANCE

Mortgage advice and negotiation companies for non-French speakers advertise in the *French Property News* and *Focus on France* property magazines and you can also contact them at the property shows organised in the UK by these magazines. (See Chapter 4.)

Abbey National France have five regional offices and bilingual staff to take you step by step through the mortgage process. Visit the English website (www.abbey-national.fr).

The following are loans (*prêts*), some of which are subject to certain conditions, for buying or improving properties in France:

Le prêt conventionné (PC)

This is a general purpose loan for new and old property purchase, heating installation work, extensions providing an additional **habitable** area of at least 14 m^2, and renovation/restoration work. The property must be the main residence and occupied (within a year after any work has been completed) for at least eight months a year.

Banks offering the *PC* have signed an agreement with the state not to exceed the maximum possible interest rate, for **variable** interest rate loans, determined and fixed for 12 months, annually, by the Credit Foncier de France. Fixed interest rate loans are also available The usual repayment periods are between five and 25 years.

The maximum loan amount depends on income. *PC* loans offer lower interest rates than personal bank loans (see below), which are over a shorter period.

Crédit immobilier bancaire (bank property loan)

This loan applies to any property purchase and/or renovation/restoration in excess of €21,500. In practice this will cover nearly all property purchases.

There is no upper limit, provided of course that the bank is confident that you can meet repayments and accepts your application. First and/or second home purchases can be financed and current interest rates with many banks are extremely attractive. Repayment periods are in general up to 15 years.

For renovation/restoration work, funds are usually paid directly to the companies concerned against invoices or stage-payment demands.

Prêts bancaires personnels (personal bank loans)

These short-term loans (from two to five years), unlike the *PC*, can be used for second homes. The interest rate is high and the amount that can be borrowed is limited to €21,500. This is the loan to use if you plan DIY improvements to a second home as there is no obligation to use professional building companies.

Subject to satisfactory credit standing a bank offer can be made to you immediately, with the funds available after a fortnight. You also have a seven-day cooling off period, even if you accept the offer immediately, meaning that you can cancel your acceptance within this period if, for example, you come across a better offer elsewhere.

Some banks offer flexible credit *spécial travaux* in addition to the fixed amount for the personal loan, giving you the possibility (without any obligation) of drawing on extra funds if your original budget proves to be insufficient. The interest rate will usually be higher for this privilege. This is worth considering if you are not in a hurry to complete the work or you plan to do it in stages.

Le prêt pass-travaux

If you have a modest income as a salaried employee, perhaps just starting your career in France, with a private, non-agricultural French company, you are entitled to a loan of up to €9,600 at a reduced interest rate and up to 10 years to finance renovation/restoration work. The work must be carried out by a professional to a main residence.

Not unreasonably, it won't cover the cost of putting in kitchen appliances or a bath, but redecoration, tiling, heating and even some extension work are possible. If you're single and live outside the Paris area your annual income must not exceed €11,369.65. For a couple with no children, the annual income limit is €15,156.48. In the Paris area the respective figures are €13,263.06 and €17,049.90. Funds are released upon presentation of invoices less than three months old for work done. An advance can be made against presentation of an accepted estimate. Companies with over 10 employees are attached to a local organisation (*l'organisme collecteur*) which handles applications. If you are in a smaller company phone 01 44 85 81 00 to obtain details of the local organisation which should receive your application.

Loans for gas and electrical work

Loans are available at preferential interest rates for certain gas (GDF) and electricity (EDF) heating installations, modernisations or renovations.

Gas

Loans are obtained through the Pétrofigaz bank (a subsidiary of the GDF) for first or second homes. The work must be carried out by a professional gas fitter. If the gas fitter is on the Gaz de France list (phone the GDF on +33 (0)810 140 150 or Pétrofigaz on +33 (0)1 40 17 55 95 or contact your local GDF office) they will assist you with your loan application, making sure it is done correctly as they will be paid directly by the bank after the work has been completed. There are three loan types:

1. The 'first installation' (*1er équipement Gaz*) for conversion to natural gas or for a first-time gas installation. Between €3,000 and €7,000 are loaned at no more than 2.95 per cent.

2. The *prêt Renovgaz* for modernisation of an existing natural gas installation. Between €1,200 and €5,000 are loaned at 6.95 per cent with repayment periods from 30 to 85 months.

3. The *prêt Aquagaz*. This is an interest-free loan for households with gas heaters who want to replace their hot water system by a natural gas powered system. Loans are between €1,500 and €2,250.

Electricity

Similarly, the EDF works with a finance company, COFIDIS, for loans. Properties must be at least five years old and the new installation or renovation must account for at least 50 per cent of the household's heating consumption. Approved professional electricians who have been awarded the Promotelec Habitat seal of approval must be used. (Phone the EDF on +33 (0) 810 126 126 or Projelec on +33 (0) 820 363 363 or contact your local EDF office).

The electrician will help you fill out your application to COFIDIS, who pays them directly when the work is completed. The cost of heating insulating materials can be included in the loan application. Loans can be arranged for

€1,500 to €8,000 and from 12 to 48 months. Above €8,000 and up to €21,500 COFIDIS may grant you a loan, but at higher interest rates.

If you are replacing or improving the heating system in a property over 15 years old which is your main home **and** you have extremely modest income you may be entitled to a grant from the national agency for home improvements (*l'Agence Nationale pour l'Amélioration de l'Habitat* or *ANAH*). Visit the French website at www.anah.fr or contact the local *Direction Départementale de l'Equipement* office for full details.

Solar energy

A relatively small state subsidy in relation to the cost of solar heating installations, the *prime COMBI*, is available: up to €2,670. Visit the French website at www.ademe.fr/particuliers/ and click on 'Plan Soleil' for details. Local subsidies, however, in certain areas, *départements* and *regions* can supplement this. Tax relief (see below) may also apply, making a heavy investment less onerous.

Store finance offers

Large stores' easy payment terms for materials and appliances make good sense, with three or four no interest equal monthly instalments, or 10 equal monthly payments at a cost of just 1 per cent or pay-later terms. Longer credit periods, however, through the store's outside finance company, have higher interest rates than bank loans. The same applies to credit terms offered by swimming pool manufacturers and installers. You may be tempted because the loan is easier to obtain, but you will pay more. Go to your bank.

VAT (*TVA*)

In September 1999 VAT was reduced from 20.6 per cent, to 5.5 per cent on most work carried out by a professional contractor to habitable properties (*logements réservés à l'habitation*) over two years old. The reduced rate, which also applies to materials and much of the equipment used, was extended in December 2003 for a further two years, but may not continue indefinitely.

The reduced rate applies to properties as follows:

◆ All properties (first and second homes, rented or vacant accommodation) plus **existing** adjacent rooms and areas such as attics, balconies, cellars, garages and terraces. If under 50 per cent of the property, excluding the adjacent rooms and areas, is used for business or industrial use before work begins the entire property is still liable for the reduced rate. Otherwise only the existing habitable parts of the property have the reduced rate.

◆ Pathways from the property to public roads, border walls and fencing and excavation work for laying on gas, electricity, telephone and water services.

◆ Business or industrial premises over two years old converted to habitable accommodation. Major redesign work including new construction work is, however, excluded, such as a factory converted to apartments.

The reduced rate applies to improvement, conversion, renovation, fitting and maintenance work carried out and invoiced by a professional and for the basic materials required and supplied and invoiced by the **same** professional:

◆ Plumbing renovation and repairs, electrical work, re-flooring, re-roofing, wall repairs and *ravalement*, decorating, fitting bathrooms, new windows, partition wall demolitions, etc. Maintenance and repairs to all items installed at 5.5 per cent VAT rating are also included.

◆ Strengthening or repairs to foundations.

◆ Attic conversions to habitable space including new floors and new rafters or beams if these are necessary.

◆ Fitted kitchens and bathrooms. (Equipment that is not permanently fixed to property walls and floors, such as free-standing floor units, is VAT rated at 19.6 per cent, as are basic appliances such as cookers, ovens, dishwashers, washing machines and refrigerators.)

◆ Supply and installation of alarm systems.

◆ Fixed heating appliances and hot water tanks. (Mobile radiators and other heaters are liable for 19.6 per cent VAT.)

The standard VAT rate of 19.6 per cent applies to all **creation** of new floor areas such as extensions, building a terrace, converting an existing terrace to a covered veranda, excavating a cellar – whatever is considered by the tax authorities to be new construction work. **Existing** attics (as seen above) which are to be converted do not fall into this category.

TAXATION

Several construction and property taxes apply to residences. Note that land tax (*taxe foncière*) in particular may vary considerably between adjacent municipalities and should be taken into account when buying property.

Taxe foncière (land tax)

This is payable annually by all property owners (not tenants) to the community. New constructions, rebuilding work (you've been authorised to demolish the ruin in the garden and have planning permission to build a summer kitchen) and extensions are exempt for two years. The local tax office must be advised of all conversion, construction and improvements to the property including any new bathroom, heating and kitchen installations within three months of completion. There may be exceptions to this temporary exemption if you have not used a *prêt conventionné*.

Permanent exemption applies if you are over 75 or are between 65 and 75 with limited income and if you live in the property as your main home (*résidence principale*). If you are unable to rent a property which is normally let, for at least three months, and you are not living there, payment of the tax can be postponed.

Taxe d'habitation (community tax)

This tax is established at the beginning of each year and is payable by the person (not necessarily the owner) who occupies the property. It is based on the letting value of the property, and new improvements/fixed constructions such as a permanent swimming pool, fitted kitchen, veranda, etc., and the overall habitable area of the property are all taken into account.

Widows or widowers and people over 60 and disabled persons all with low incomes, subject to a means test, are exempt. A reduction in the tax applies if you have living with you your children, up to the age of 25, who attend college or university and/or handicapped or over 70-year-old parents who have low incomes. If your own income is modest, subject to a means test, you may be entitled to a reduction.

Taxe locale d'équipement (town planning tax)

This tax is levied in all communities with a population of over 10,000, certain parts of the Ile-de-France area and in many smaller municipalities.

It is a town planning tax payable by the property owner in two equal parts, 18 and 36 months after planning permission has been granted or you have given notice of the work planned (*déclaration de travaux*), for construction or extension work. Ask the local authorities – town hall or the DDE – for details of the rate applied in your area and whether you will be liable to pay any other taxes such as environment tax (*taxe départementale des espaces naturels sensibles*) and road taxes (*participation aux financements des voies nouvelles*).

Le credit d'impôt

If you pay income tax in France you may be eligible for some forms of tax rebate. Up until the end of December 2005 tax rebate is possible on the purchase cost of certain heating and insulating material and equipment, provided it has been installed in your main residence which is over two years old by the professional contractor who also supplied it. The installation cost is not taken into account.

The rebate applies to:

- wall heating insulation panels (fibreglass, polystyrene, etc.)
- wood and PVC shutters
- lagging (*calorifugeage*) material

◆ thermostats

◆ double-glazing

◆ boilers, stoves and fireplaces powered by renewable energy sources or materials – solar power, wood and other natural combustible matter

◆ heating pumps

◆ hammam baths and saunas.

The tax rebate equals 15 per cent of the purchase cost and is limited, for purchases in the period January 2003 to 31 December 2005, to €4,000 for a single person and €8,000 for a couple who are taxed jointly. Additional, smaller allowances are made for children. The rebate applies if the 15 per cent amount exceeds the income tax you pay in the year when the purchase is made.

Robien's tax relief measure

The French Housing Minister's recent measure is of interest if you buy an old property as an investment which must be renovated *aux caractéristiques de décence* (to a decent standard) before you can put it on the rental market. The conditions are that the property must be rented out for a minimum period of nine years within a year of its purchase and not to a member of your family included in your annual income return (*Déclaration des Revenus*). So the renovation work needs to be put in hand promptly.

Monthly rents are government controlled. The Paris, Côte d'Azur and French Alps area near Geneva 'ceiling' is €14.4 per m²; urban areas of over 50,000 people, €9.4 per m² and other areas, €6.3 per m². For example, an apartment near the Franco-Swiss border with 60 m² habitable area can be rented for up to €864 a month. The tax advantages allow you to deduct from your rental returns declaration on your tax form 8 per cent of the property's purchase price **and** renovation costs for the first five years and 2.5 per cent for the following four years.

Useful vocabulary

calorifugeage	lagging material
paiement en trois ou quatre fois, sans frais	three or four interest-free payments
règlement reporté	deferred payment
taux fixes, taux variables	fixed interest rate, variable interest rate
versements échelonnés	stage payments

Useful Websites

BUYING

www.french-property-news.com
Properties for sale details online. Magazine subscription details.

www.worldofpropertyexhibition.com
Properties for sale details online, with detailed descriptions and colour photos. *Focus on France* magazine subscription details.

www.fnaim.com
The website, in French only, of the National Federation of Estate Agents (FNAIM). Federation estate agent members throughout France and independent valuers (*experts immobiliers*). Do not confuse *experts immobiliers* with technical construction experts.

www.century21.fr
700 franchised estate agents. Colour photos.

www.laforet.com
400 franchised estate agents. No photos.

www.erafrance.com
300 estate agents. Colour photos.

www.orpi.com
Property advertisements in French and English.

www.immonot.com
The French notaries' information site. Conveyancing costs in English. Property for sale photos, but no English descriptions.

www.immoprix.com
French notaries' survey, by size, town, area, *département* and region of average prices, for old and new apartments and old and new houses sold over previous 12 months. Not in English, but easy to visit.

www.seloger.com
Property advertisements in English with 360° virtual reality visits. French information on finance and costs and a directory of building (including renovation and restoration) specialists.

www.logic-immo.com
French text *LogicImmo* property advertisements magazine, some with photos. Updated every three weeks. Link to www.demeuresetchateaux.fr site, in French and English, for luxury residences, some ripe for renovation.

www.pap.fr
The *De Particulier à Particulier* (property owners not using estate agents) magazine site with property descriptions in English and some photos.

RENOVATING

www.pagesjaunes.fr
The French Yellow Pages online.

www.theanglophonebook.com
Côte d'Azur Yellow Pages directory, in English, of English-speaking businesses, including property/real estate, and construction and building.

www.batimat.com
Details in French and English of the International Building Materials and Technologies Exhibition held every two years in Paris.

www.batirama.com and **www.capeb.fr**
For French speakers. Up-to-date information for the building trades.

www.huisclos.fr
Informative site with diagrams, colour photos and product descriptions, in French only, for this national company's range of aluminium, PVC and wood double-glazed windows.

www.kpark.fr
Similar range of products to Huisclos, also available nationally. This site shows quality certification labels (*labels de qualité*) and also has product information, in French only, under '*un peu de technique*'.

www.sogal.com
Excellent multi-language site with clear diagrams of fitted bedroom and cupboard possibilities. Addresses of their regional shops. Email details for an estimate and make sure you stipulate your French address.

www.archea.fr
Fitted bedroom and cupboard designs. List of boutiques throughout France.

www.quadro.fr

Illustrated site, in English, showing their fitted bedroom and cupboard designs. Boutiques only in Lyon, Ile de France, Rouen and Oise areas.

www.hexdalle.com

Specialist manufacturer of rubber-based shock absorbing flooring for games and activity areas. French and English text product descriptions.

All the seven following materials and/or DIY suppliers' websites (from www.bricorama.fr to www.gedimat.fr) are in French only, with the exception of Lapeyre which has online product ordering in French and English. Castorama also has online ordering, but not in English. Leroy Merlin compare similar products in their ranges for you. Lively and updated regularly, all sites have technical advice on use of products and current best-buys.

www.bricorama.fr

www.castorama.fr

www.leroymerlin.fr

www.mr-bricolage.fr

www.weldom.com

www.lapeyre.fr

www.gedimat.fr

www.qualibat.com

French only. Approved building companies and company information.

www.qualifelec.fr

French only. Approved electrical installation companies.

www.gesec.fr

French only, although English is planned. The GESEC federation is the voice for 240 heating, electrical, air-conditioning and bathroom installation professionals throughout most of France.

www.legens.com

Authentic old materials, including fireplaces. English descriptions.

www.origines.com
Auctioneers of old materials. English descriptions and photos. Order their catalogue online.

www.securiflame.fr
In French only. Cleaning and maintenance products for fireplaces.

www.zodiacpools.com
Comprehensive site in English with detailed product explanations and descriptions for this renowned manufacturer's range of self-assembly pools.

www.abrideal.com
Swimming pool hatch roofs. Attractive and informative. In English.

www.termite.com.fr
Click on '*carte métropolitaine*' for infestation levels in France and click on '*carte départementale*' for areas where the local authorities impose surveys. For general information, in English, the American site www.termite.com is useful.

www.edf.fr
The English site for individual homeowners is not yet in English, but keep trying, it will be. Meanwhile the *maison virtuelle* will give you good tips on what (watt) to use, electrically, round the house.

www.gazdefrance.com
French national gas company site (only in French). Click on '*Dolce Vita*' and then use the animated visit round the house for advice.

www.ademe.fr/particuliers/
In French only. Includes general advice for homeowners on cost-effective energy management.

FINANCE

www.abbey-national.fr
Mortgage information, in French and English.

www.caixabank.fr
Attractive loans for properties. In French only.

Further Reading

BOOKS

An Orderly Man, Dirk Bogarde (Chatto and Windus)
A Year in Provence, Peter Mayle (Pan)
Buying a Property in France, Clive Kristen (How To Books)
Buy to Let in France, Clive Kristen (How To Books)
Starting & Running a B & B in France, Denorah Hunt (How To Books)
The Best Places to Buy a Home in France, Joe Laredo (Survival Books)

ENGLISH LANGUAGE NEWSPAPERS AND MAGAZINES

The News, SARL Brussac, 225 route d'Angoulême, BP 4042, 24004
   Perigueux, France. National and regional news for residents and lovers of
   France. Property, financial and building services advertisements.
   Monthly.
The Riviera Times, 8 avenue Jean Moulin, 06340 Drap, France. Local and
   national news and property articles. Some property, financial and building
   service advertisements. Monthly.
The Riviera Reporter, 56 Chemin de Provence, 06250 Mougins, France.
   Competes with *The Riviera Times*.
Focus on France, Outbound Publishing, 1 Commercial Road, Eastbourne,
   East Sussex BN21 3XQ. Every two months.
French Property News, 6 Burgess Mews, Wimbledon, London SW19 1UF.
   Monthly.
Living France Magazine, Archant life, Cumberland House, Oriel Road,
   Cheltenham, Glos. GLSU 1BB. Includes property section with articles
   and advertisements. Monthly.

Index

access, 23, 24, 62, 68, 70
aeration, 55, 64, 66, 90, 93, 127, 135
air-conditioning, 57, 109
alarm systems, 92, 100, 111, 112, 156, 167
anti-frost depths, 4, 55
architects, 3, 35, 45, 58, 68, 69, 73, 75, 77, 86, 97, 125, 153, 158, 159, 161
architects' plans, 45
architectural styles, 44
asbestos, 35, 92, 96, 97, 134
auction, 120
authenticity, 35, 70, 120
awnings, 141 .

barbecues, 46, 134
barns, 134
beams, 122, 167
blue-print, 74
boundaries, 47
brick types, 55
Britanny longère renovation 8, 9
building surface, 49
builders, 58, 74, 154, 155
builders' merchants, 148, 150, 157
bungalow, 134, 135
business premises, 4, 62, 167

cabinet maker, 76
cables, 136
Carrez's Law, 33, 40
carpets, 149
casement windows, 90
cements, 69, 70, 87
chalet renovation, 13, 14
chimneys, 109, 110, 149
clay floors, 9, 12
climate, xiv, 57, 136
cold welding, 113

community tax, 168
conservation area properties, 48
country houses, 73, 74
cracks, 127, 136, 151
crazy paving, 142

decorating materials, 126, 127, 128, 129, 130
decorating walls/ceilings, 127, 128, 130, 131
demolition work, 34, 97, 158
design, 74
dictionary, xv
DIY, 83, 86, 89, 99, 123, 125, 148, 151, 158, 159, 164
double-glazing, 59, 64
down payments, 161, 162
drainage, 36, 116, 143

EDF, 57
Electrical heating appliances, 106, 107
electricity tariff, 101
electricity safety regulations, 104
entrances, 69
estimates, 74, 77, 80, 81, 82, 86, 87, 88, 96, 105, 159, 160, 161
euro symbol, xv
exhibitions, 126, 127, 157
extensions, 45, 141

fees, 42
fibre-glass, 130
finance, 159
fitted bathrooms, 86, 167
fitted kitchens, 14, 167, 169
fitted kitchen companies, 78, 82

fixtures and fittings, 76
floor units, 80
flooring, 65, 70, 71, 86, 156
FNAIM, xiii, 37, 40
foundations, 35, 54, 58, 134, 141, 142, 167
fungi/fungicide, 67, 95, 100
furniture stores, 77

garages/garage doors, 47, 67, 68
gas tariff, 108
GDF, 57
generator, 111
guarantees, 54, 56, 57, 58, 59, 75, 76, 90, 96, 104, 110, 123, 126, 134, 136, 138, 141, 150, 153, 155, 156, 162
glue, 94, 130, 131, 142, 148
guttering, 93, 149, 150

habitable area, 62
habitable area (letting), 65
half-timbering, 10, 12, 148
hammam bath, 84
hardware shops, 150
hard water, 114
heating appliances, 57, 65
holiday homes, 99
hot-water tanks, 110

insecticides, 96, 100
insulation, ceilings, 53, 56, 57, 63, 64, 65, 130
insulation, sound, 56, 63, 64, 168
insulation, veranda, 59
insulation, walls, 53, 55, 63, 64, 66, 130
insurance, 89, 90, 100, 153, 154
interior decorator, 125

intrusion detectors, 112

kitchen renovations, 9, 12, 15

land tax, 168
ladders, 93
lead-content paint, 35, 92, 97, 98
leaks, 67, 113
letting, 4, 99, 135, 170
listed property, 48
loans, 163, 164, 165

maintenance products, 147
marble, 89
materials, choice of, 74, 161
mezzanine, 77
mortgages, 162

national estate agents, 34
notary, 36, 37, 41, 42

open-plan, 69
old tiles, renovation of, 12, 120
original (authentic) materials, 49, 120, 121
outlook, 24, 28, 133
outside kitchens, 15, 134
owner's association, 45

paints, 129
paint brushes, 129, 130
parquet, 71, 148
partition walls, 56, 57, 65, 69, 74, 89, 127, 151
patio, 58
payment terms, 157, 161, 166
pergola, 142
pipes, 113, 115, 137
planning limits, 34, 35
plumber, 113
polycarbonate, 134
polyester, 134, 138
polyethylene, 115
polyurethane, 113, 129
pool filters, 138
pool shells, liners, 138, 139

pool-houses, 134
property advertisements, 29, 30, 61
property dealers, 38
property magazine subscriptions, 29, 30
property prices, 21, 25
protective clothing, 152, 158
Provence farmhouse renovation, 15
purchase fees, 3
PVC, 100
PVC windows, 113, 115, 134, 136, 138

rebates, 57
recuperating old material, 13, 18, 120
refunds, 115
refurbishment, 118, 119
rental premises, 4
replica materials, 118, 121
re-flooring, 108
re-roofing, 18, 56, 92, 167
risk areas, 35
Robien's tax relief, 170
roof insulation, 15, 17, 63
roofing materials, 134
room sizes, 32, 77, 78, 84

sales mandate, 36
sauna, 84
scaffolding, 123
self-assembly, 83, 100, 135, 136
semi-basements, 67, 68
septic tanks, 149
sewerage, 116
shade, 41
shutters, 90, 92, 98, 99 118, 121
soft water, 104
solar panels, 110
sole agents, 30, 32
special paints, 128
specialised estate agents, 34
split-level floors, 69
stage payments, 74, 162, 163
staircases, 62, 69, 121, 122

stonework, 118
stone fireplaces, 120
stripping, 127
sun terrace, 140
surveillance, 112
surveyor, 66, 95, 96, 97
synthetic fabrics, 131

taps, 84, 87
tax guidance, 4, 5
tax liability, 49, 62, 139
tax rebate, 84, 169, 170
taxes, 42, 168, 169
teak, 89, 148
terraces, 20, 46, 120, 136, 141, 142, 168
thermal insulation, 58
tiles, 58, 70, 71, 87, 89, 93, 108, 118, 120, 121, 141, 142, 149, 156
town gas, 108
town planning regulations, 45
town planning tax, 169

undercoats, 128
urban planning, 36

VAT, 82, 86, 155, 159, 161, 162, 166
ventilation, 86
veranda, 53, 54, 58, 59, 141, 168

wall coatings, 122
wall cupboards, 78,
wallpapers, 130
walls, 35, 46, 55, 63, 64, 66, 67, 70, 74, 78, 86, 89, 96, 97, 109, 118, 122, 123, 126, 129, 130, 135
waterproofing, 64, 67, 69, 93, 94, 120, 128, 129, 148
water supply, 36, 114
windows, 65, 69, 90, 133, 134, 156
wood rot, 100
work tops, 80, 121